ENVIRO-CAPITALISTS

The Political Economy Forum
Sponsored by the Political Economy Research Center (PERC)
Series Editor: Terry L. Anderson

Land Rights: The 1990s' Property Rights Rebellion
    Edited by Bruce Yandle

The Political Economy of Customs and Culture: Informal Solutions to the Commons Problem
    Edited by Terry L. Anderson and Randy T. Simmons

The Political Economy of the American West
    Edited by Terry L. Anderson and Peter J. Hill

Property Rights and Indian Economies
    Edited by Terry L. Anderson

Public Lands and Private Rights: The Failure of Scientific Management
    By Robert H. Nelson

Taking the Environment Seriously
    Edited by Roger E. Meiners and Bruce Yandle

Wildlife in the Marketplace
    Edited by Terry L. Anderson and Peter J. Hill

The Privatization Process: A Worldwide Perspective
    Edited by Terry L. Anderson and Peter J. Hill

Enviro-Capitalists: Doing Good While Doing Well
    By Terry L. Anderson and Donald R. Leal

ENVIRO-CAPITALISTS

Doing Good While Doing Well

Terry L. Anderson
and
Donald R. Leal

ROWMAN & LITTLEFIELD PUBLISHERS, INC.
Lanham • New York • Boulder • Oxford

ROWMAN & LITTLEFIELD PUBLISHERS, INC.

Published in the United States of America
by Rowman & Littlefield Publishers, Inc.
4720 Boston Way, Lanham, Maryland 20706

12 Hid's Copse Road
Cummor Hill, Oxford OX2 9JJ, England

British Library Cataloguing in Publication Information Available

Library of Congress Cataloging-in-Publication Data

Anderson, Terry Lee, 1946–
    Enviro-capitalists : doing good while doing well / Terry L.
Anderson and Donald R. Leal.
        p.   cm.—(The political economy forum)
    Includes bibliographical references and index.
    ISBN 0-8476-8381-8 (alk. paper).—ISBN 0-8476-8382-6 (pbk. :
alk. paper)
    1. Environmental protection—Economic aspects—United States.
2. Sustainable development—United States.   3. Capitalism—
Environmental Aspects—United States.   4. Entrepreneurship—United
States.   I. Leal, Donald.   II. Title.   III. Series.
HC110.E5A6663   1997
363.7'00973—dc21   96-40115
                                                                CIP

ISBN 0–8476–8381–8 (cloth : alk. paper)
ISBN 0–8476–8382–6 (pbk. : alk. paper)

Printed in the United States of America

Contents

Acknowledgments

In 1991 we published *Free Market Environmentalism*, which laid out the theory for market solutions to environmental problems. Since then, we discovered that this theory is brought to life by hundreds of environmental entrepreneurs who have made free market environmentalism a reality. We thank all of those featured in this book, especially Tom Bourland and Brent Haglund, for stimulating our thinking on this subject. To those whose stories remain untold because of our ignorance, we beg your indulgence. Hopefully this book will help us discover and appreciate your contributions to improving our environment. We thank John Baden who made us aware of the adjective-adverb combination in the subtitle.

Projects like this always require financial support from "idea entrepreneurs." For this we thank the Earhart Foundation, the Scaife Foundation, and the M. J. Murdock Charitable Trust. Their funding made it possible for the research. We also thank the PERC staff including Monica Lane Guenther, Michelle Johnson, Pam Malyurek, and Dianna Rienhart. Research assistance and ideas from Holly Lippke Fretwell, Mike Houser, and Pam Snyder are also greatly appreciated. Without the staff, we would still be just thinking about this project.

Finally, we thank our families for their patience in enduring our moods and time commitments. Thanks to Janet, Sarah, and Peter, and Dorothy, and the "Brittanys," Max, Molly, and Maggie (and of course, her seven pups).

Chapter 1

Nature's Entrepreneurs

We have our idealists, inventors, innovators and organizers all
around us, and in a vast mechanism of economic and social change
there is work for all kinds to do . . .

—Jonathan Hughes, *The Vital Few*

In his book *The Vital Few*, Jonathan Hughes (1986) describes the entrepreneurs of the late nineteenth and early twentieth centuries who unleashed America's industrial power. Names like Rockefeller, Vanderbilt, Carnegie, Ford, and Morgan lead the cast of characters. In some cases these "vital few" invented new products or production techniques, but mostly they amassed capital, contracted with other input owners, and developed marketing strategies that lowered the cost of products and increased profits. In recent times, industrialists may have fallen from the list of the vital few, replaced by electronic-information gurus like Bill Gates or media moguls like Ted Turner, but the required entrepreneurial skills remain basically the same.

It is impossible to predict the frontiers on which the next wave of entrepreneurs will leave their mark. If such predictions were easy, we might all enjoy the riches of successful innovation. Not surprisingly, therefore, business schools around the country, trying to teach entrepreneurship, are continually frustrated because switching on imagination and innovation is hard. Lacking any theory that explains entrepreneurship, about all that we can do is search the case studies of successful and unsuccessful entrepreneurs to identify similarities. This search consistently reveals that vision alone is only part of what entrepreneurs possess and is of little value without other business acumen. Those who see opportunities also must be able to seize them by coordinating complementary inputs. For example, inventing the reaper was only the first step for Cyrus McCormick. To get his invention into the

1

hands of farmers and make a profit, McCormick had to contract with owners of capital to produce the machine and with salesmen to market it. Understanding entrepreneurship requires investigating these latter steps as well as the initial inventions.

This book investigates what it takes to be a successful entrepreneur in the environmental arena. If we were to compile a list of the vital few from the environmental history books, it might be headed with names like Audubon, Leopold, and Muir. As entrepreneurs, these men recognized the value of the natural world at a time when most people saw nature's frontier as a wilderness to be tamed. Of these early entrepreneurs, however, only Aldo Leopold saw the importance of linking the conservation movement to entrepreneurship, with all the trappings of finance, contracting, marketing, and, even profits.

Unfortunately, many of today's environmentalists have not picked up where Leopold left off. His entrepreneurial spirit has given way to political opportunism. Instead of business acumen, the vital few in the environmental movement understand politics, lobbying, and fundraising as the tools to achieve their political objectives. The headquarters for most major groups are located in Washington, D.C., and the personnel spend their time in the halls of Congress rather than in the wilds of nature.

The campaign to "save" the African elephant illustrates how political and financial agendas can overtake environmental realism. Though more than 1 million elephants roam southern Africa, environmental leaders of groups such as the Humane Society of the United States and the World Wildlife Fund declared elephants an endangered species and instituted fund-raising campaigns, publicized with vivid pictures of slaughtered elephants, tusks removed by chain saws. They raised millions of dollars to promote a ban on trade in ivory, although many African conservationists believed this would only further drive up the price of ivory and increase poaching.[1] Rather than channeling their efforts into the direct protection of elephant habitat, these leaders politicized the elephant issue and motivated politicians and bureaucrats to ban trade in elephant products through CITES (Convention on International Trade in Endangered Species). They gave little consideration to the incentives faced by African natives who directly bear the costs of living with the elephants. These people, many of whom live at subsistence levels, are being asked to preserve habitat, let their crops be destroyed, and perhaps even be killed to save elephants because westerners living in comfort thousands of miles across the ocean think it is a good idea. These political entrepreneurs demand the protection of elephants but place the burden of that protection on the backs of those who can least afford it. In the end, the campaign to "save" African elephants by banning trade in ivory filled the coffers of western environmental groups. Unfortunately, it reduced the potential for Africans to live in harmony with elephants because it prevented the indigenous population from profiting from good stewardship.

For the past twenty-five years, environmental policy in the United States and around the world has relied on command-and-control regulations. A plethora of laws governing water, air, public lands, and endangered species used the stick as opposed to the carrot to achieve environmental ends. Certainly, some regulation was necessary, and the environment has improved. But growing acrimony has forced the environmental community to consider whether they might have slighted the carrot in the policy process. Hence, discussions of economic incentives and market-based approaches permeate current environmental policy discussions. But even these discussions often assume that the incentives must emanate from the political sector.

This book considers an alternative approach—enviro-capitalism—that begins when environmental entrepreneurs discover new opportunities for improving environmental quality and then figure out how to produce it in the private sector. Enviro-capitalists are entrepreneurs using business tools to preserve open space, develop wildlife habitat, save endangered species, and generally improve environmental quality. These entrepreneurs are meeting the growing demand for recreational and environmental amenities. To do this, enviro-capitalists must invent new products, attract venture capital, contract with resource owners, and market their products. The enviro-capitalist encourages fee hunting to reward landowners for bearing the cost of providing habitat for wild animals; buys endangered species habitat instead of lobbying for regulations that restrict the use of private lands; and leases water to increase instream flows, rather than seeking legislation to limit water use by irrigators. In meeting each of these human demands, enviro-capitalists also benefit the environment.

The stories in this book support the growing realization that markets can be a powerful force in the environmental movement. Market-based incentives have become a common approach in both the private and public sectors. Corporations are searching for ways to increase profits in environmentally friendly ways. Policy makers are facing the reality that a cleaner environment comes at an increasingly higher cost. By harnessing market forces as enviro-capitalists do, we can achieve environmental ends at a lower cost.

Environmental entrepreneurship, however, is not a panacea. It will not solve all environmental problems. The examples in this book focus mainly on land, wildlife, and water issues because they involve resources more amenable to contracting and marketing. Enviro-capitalists have not solved global environmental problems. But this approach illustrates how entrepreneurial solutions to small, local problems can provide the foundation for thinking innovatively about bigger problems.

With rising incomes, the demand for environmental amenities grows. The question is who will meet those demands, politicians or enviro-capitalists. The former seem to be the accepted norm in a world where environmental crises dominate headlines. The vital few discussed in this book provide evidence of what can be accomplished by harnessing the incentives of the marketplace. To set the stage, we offer three examples of enviro-capitalists at work.

More Than Paper Profits

Tom Bourland, wildlife biologist and entrepreneur, preaches that the market can be wildlife's best ally. He believes that the growing demand for wildlife and recreation provides landowners with powerful incentives to produce more wildlife habitat and more recreational opportunities. And he should know, having turned wildlife into a money-maker for International Paper (IP), one of the largest timber producers in the United States.

In the early 1980s, Bourland became a wildlife manager of 1.2 million acres of IP's timber-producing land in its mid-south region, including parts of Texas, Louisiana, and Arkansas. When he joined the company, its wildlife and recreation program was not designed to generate income but rather to keep neighbors happy, appease environmentalists, and stem the rising tide of government regulations placed on private timber owners. Bourland was hired as a token wildlife biologist to operate within this agenda, but he was quickly frustrated—the bottom line on the financial statement was driven by timber production.

Recognizing the importance of the profit motive, Bourland locked his entrepreneurial radar onto the relationship between wildlife and IP's financial statements. He noted the growing demand for hunting, fishing, and recreation, as well as consumers' willingness to pay for quality experiences.[2] But he also saw that the company was receiving nothing for the use of these amenities. Bourland's environmental agenda had to give way to new realities. To respond to these realities, the company's wildlife and recreation program had to earn its way by charging user fees of those enjoying the amenities on IP's lands.

Charging fees for recreation represented a bold move for a timber company because it was bucking tradition. In the rural townships of Louisiana, Bourland's home state, local people were accustomed to hunting, fishing, and camping for free on IP's lands. Some did not take kindly to having to pay. Indeed, some regional managers at IP worried that they would be the ones facing the wrath of a disgruntled public. According to IP's chairman and chief executive, John Georges, "There were times when some executives were asking, 'Is it worth it—should we be doing this?' " (quoted in Killian 1991).

Despite local objections, IP proceeded with the change, spurred by several factors. Besides evidence of growing recreational demand, increasing abuse on IP's open lands was costing the company dearly. Litter, arson, and off-road traffic were major problems. Also, wildlife populations were declining from years of poaching and excessive legal hunting. Hunters were complaining about too little game and too many people.

Bourland and other supporters of fees at IP argued that revenues from wildlife and recreation would more than offset the additional costs of monitoring IP's lands and improving conditions for wildlife. They believed that fees for land use provided an effective strategy that would create stronger incentives for users to care for the land. A major part of the fee program included selling multiyear land leases to hunting clubs. Under the lease arrangement, clubs have a personal stake in stewardship of "their" areas. Bourland believed that clubs would monitor land use, limit hunting pressure, and cooperate with wildlife managers, all of which would add to the members' enjoyment of the recreation on IP property and lower the company's costs.

IP had already made substantial investments in experimental wildlife management programs and knew the potential for integrating wildlife management with timber programs. In 1957 the company established its 16,000-acre Southlands Experimental Forest near Bainbridge, Georgia. This forest served as a proving ground for management techniques that harmonize timber production and the needs of wildlife while earning profits from recreation. Exemplifying the innovative techniques pioneered at Southlands were experiments with prescribed burning. Fire is an important tool in the management of southern pine forests. Because the pines are fire-resistant, periodic burning reduces competitive undergrowth and thereby enhances timber production. Prescribed burning also benefits wildlife by promoting the growth of browse essential to white-tailed deer and bobwhite quail. Prior to the Southlands burning projects, deer, turkey, quail, and rabbit populations on the experimental forest were low. By the early 1980s, however, prescribed burning had dramatically increased populations of these species. After visiting Southlands, outdoor writer Richard Starnes (1982) concluded, "Experiments with whitetails, turkey, quail, dove, rabbits, and a host of other game and nongame species are proving that it is practical—and profitable—to manage continuous-yield tree plantations in a way that ensures the healthy proliferation of wildlife."

Under Bourland's direction, the company launched its fee-based wildlife and recreation program in 1983, emphasizing three sources for revenues: hunting club leases, daily use permits, and seasonal family permits. By 1986, the program had made dramatic strides. Revenues from recreational sales in Arkansas, Louisiana, and Texas had tripled to $2 million, and corresponding profits were an impressive 25 percent of total profits in IP's mid-south region. Fourteen hundred hunting clubs had leased 1 million acres of IP lands, more than double the amount leased by the end of 1983. The results convinced the skeptics. Bourland aptly describes the program's progress and success:

> Managed fee hunting programs are gaining acceptance among hunters seeking exclusivity, safer conditions, and abundant game. Reaction to these market dynamics is influencing International Paper Company's approach to wildlife management on approximately 2.3 million acres of land in Texas, Arkansas, and Louisiana. "Open" lands are being converted to traditional fee access programs. Market research, consumer profiles, and customary financial tests are being employed to design commercial operations aimed at promising market segments. Future emphasis will be on customer relations and profitability. (Bourland 1986, 1)

According to Bourland (1986, 2), the hunting clubs are an integral part of wildlife management because they "can provide wildlife protection, control harvest pressure, and accomplish habitat improvements to a degree not generally possible through other arrangements." In addition, a new partnership or "contract" between recreational users and the company was being formed among a growing number of clubs that gave new meaning to wildlife management. At a club's request, company biologists provided members with wildlife management guidance, survey assistance, harvest analysis, and food plot mate-rial. In return, club members restricted their hunting techniques, recorded harvests, and followed company-imposed restrictions on har-vests. By 1986, new contracts had been adopted by nearly one-third of the 1,400 hunting clubs that leased IP land.

The company also began experimenting with other recreational packages. At the upper end of the scale, IP opened the 3,000-acre Big Oak Club in East Texas. In 1986, hunters at the club paid $200 per day for lodging and guides and for the opportunity to take one buck and two doe white-tailed deer. Farther down the price scale was the 1985 opening of the 4,000-acre San Patricio Bowhunting Area. Bowhunters using the area paid $200 per season or $100 for a three-day hunt and enjoyed a success rate of 61 percent. Services provided by the company included a walk-in cooler and campsites furnished with electricity, water, tables, grills, and bathroom facilities.

Most importantly, as revenues from IP's recreational program grew, regional forest managers began managing their forests differently. In 1988, speaking to congressional staff members in Big Sky, Montana, Bourland (1988) described the new behavior of the timber owners: "Be-cause the status of wildlife affected the bottom line, the landowner bent over backwards to provide habitat for whitetail deer, wild turkey, fox, squirrel, and bobwhite quail, as well as endangered bald eagles and red-cockade woodpeckers." They left corridors of trees 100 yards wide between harvested areas through which wildlife could travel safely. They left clumps of trees uncut while younger stands next to them grew, thus creating greater age diversity. They reduced the size of cut areas and made their perimeters more irregular and therefore more attractive to a greater variety of wildlife. They did not harvest large strips of trees and shrubs along either side of streams, and they planted food plots.

These and other efforts have paid big dividends to wildlife as well as stockholders. Ten years after the inception of the program, game surveys showed that populations of deer, turkey, fox, quail, and ducks had increased substantially. Eastern wild turkey and white-tailed deer had exhibited the largest gains, increasing tenfold and fivefold, respec-tively. According to company biologists, the main reasons are better habitat and less hunting pressure. Nongame populations have also benefited. Company biologists carry out an assortment of projects to improve habitat for these species, from putting up bluebird boxes to protecting heron rookeries. Even though nongame species have no ex-plicit market, hunters, campers, anglers, and hikers are willing to pay more for a diversified recreational experience. IP's biologists continue to explore other options that would provide additional revenue for nongame species.

The 1990s have been a time of change and continued success for the program. Bourland has left IP to form a flourishing business, providing wildlife and forest management consulting for private, nonindustrial (i.e., small) timber owners in the South. In this new venture, Bourland is helping hundreds of private forest owners benefit from the years of wildlife research carried out at IP. Meanwhile, IP's wildlife and recreation program continues to grow. Nearly two-thirds of the company's more than 6 million acres in the United States are now managed profitably for wildlife and recreation. Revenues from the program reached $10 million in 1990 and are expected to double rapidly. Thirty-five thousand hunting and recreational customers now use IP lands in Arkansas, Louisiana, and Texas, and another 25,000 pay to use IP lands elsewhere in the country. On the company's timber lands in northern Maine, for example, the public pays daily fees of $3 to $6 and seasonal fees of $15 to $90 for camping, hiking, fishing, and canoeing. In the Adirondack region of New York, people lease cabin sites, paying $700 to $1000 per year.[3]

The International Paper Company's wildlife and recreation program indicates a growing trend. In the South and the East, where most of the land base is privately owned, fee-based wildlife recreation is becoming firmly established. In addition, environmental entrepreneurs are coming up with new products and services to meet new markets. Texas ranches such as the King Ranch near Corpus Christi, the Fennessey Ranch near Baytown, and the Selah Ranch near San Antonio are providing nature hikes and bird-watching tours. In the West, where there is so much free access to public lands, it is tougher for private landowners to compete, but as we shall see in chapter 4, the fee-recreation market is beginning to develop even there. Enviro-capitalists such as Tom Bourland are leading the way for new land management techniques.

Caviar from Cattle Country

The opportunities to profit from wildlife are not limited to warm, cuddly mammals, as the Glendive Chamber of Commerce has discovered. The entrepreneurial bug hit organization members during hard times and prompted them to turn demand for American caviar into a money-maker for both their town and for one of the largest freshwater fish in North America.

In 1987, Glendive, Montana, an agricultural community of 7,000 people in eastern Montana, was feeling the effects of a persistent drought and low agricultural prices. Businesses along Main Street were struggling to survive, the tax base was shrinking, and a growing backlog of community projects needed funding. Michael Carlson, president of the chamber of commerce, recalls: "I was depressed by what was happening in Glendive. I was looking for something positive."[4]

Joseph Frank Crisafulli, a successful local entrepreneur in the sprinkler irrigation business, found that positive something—paddlefish eggs. Crisafulli knew that many people came to Glendive each spring to fish the lower Yellowstone River for paddlefish, a large prehistoric fish with a long, paddlelike snout. Anglers prize the fish for their delicious white meat and their size; they grow to five feet in length and weigh as much as 120 pounds. But the Montana anglers could care less about their roe. Several tons of the eggs were being tossed on the banks of the Yellowstone as the fish were cleaned, attracting flies and rodents. Crisafulli knew that paddlefish eggs are the main source of American caviar, which sells in exclusive New York stores for between $80 and $200 per pound. Connoisseurs of the paddlefish caviar say it is comparable to Russian Sevruga, the least expensive Russian caviar from sturgeon in the Caspian Sea. Crisafulli saw paddlefish caviar from Montana as the answer to Glendive's woes.

His idea motivated action by civic-minded leaders such as Kathy Jackson, executive director of the town's chamber of commerce. When it comes to raising money for community projects, Jackson is a pro, and she took on the project with true entrepreneurial spirit.

To turn the rotting eggs into a profit, she and the members of the chamber faced two main problems. First, they needed some enticement for fishers to bring their paddlefish to a place where the roe could be collected. Because most fishers hated the job of cleaning their catch, they were paying locals $10 per fish to get it done. The chamber of commerce offered to clean paddlefish for free in return for the paddlefish eggs.

The second problem, however, was not so easy to solve because it involved politics. The Glendive Chamber of Commerce had to convince state wildlife officials and, ultimately, the state legislature to make an exception to a state law prohibiting the sale of wild game products. They had to demonstrate that allowing the chamber of commerce to sell paddlefish eggs donated by sport fishermen posed no

threat to paddlefish populations. Wildlife officials were cautious because paddlefish populations in North America began declining in the
early 1980s, due to habitat loss, pollution, and overfishing. Although
the species still exists in twenty-two states, in several southern states,
remnants remain where populations were once abundant.

United States Fish and Wildlife Service (FWS) officials were especially wary of any new trade in paddlefish caviar. With rising caviar
prices, caviar connoisseurs found a cheaper substitute in paddlefish
caviar. As the demand for paddlefish caviar increased, commercial
fishers began putting pressure on paddlefish in the South. The commercial fishing pressure, combined with poaching, forced closure of
several state fisheries. Under these circumstances, federal wildlife officials feared that promoting trade in paddlefish products would only
make it that much harder for them to protect the generally declining
resource. For this reason, the FWS favored curtailing the market for
paddlefish caviar (Schulz 1992),[5] but fortunately for Glendive, responsibility for paddlefish management resided with the state of Montana.

Getting an exception to allow trade in Montana paddlefish eggs was
made somewhat easier by three factors. First, the change offered no
financial incentive for fishers to increase their fishing efforts because
the chamber of commerce was asking them to donate, not sell, their
roe to the nonprofit organization. Second, Montana had in place a regulated sport fishery that already lent itself to monitoring and controlling fishing pressure. Fishers must purchase tags to fish for paddlefish
and must affix a tag to each fish caught. At the time the program
began, each fisher was limited to two tags per season. The use of tags
allowed wildlife officials to track closely the number of paddlefish
taken. By requiring that the chamber of commerce take eggs only from
tagged fish, the Montana Department of Fish, Wildlife, and Parks
could limit the amount of caviar marketed. Third, the Montana paddlefish fishery was under no threat of decline. Basing their conclusions on
live capture and harvest data collected over a decade, state biologists
were on record as saying that both Fort Peck and Lake Sakakawea (the
latter shared with North Dakota) had "stable, healthy populations."[6]
Unlike many other rivers, Yellowstone's fishery is sustainable because
it is under no threat from pollution, and spawning habitat is relatively
intact.

Against this backdrop state wildlife officials and state legislators
were convinced Montana's paddlefish population would not be jeop-
ardized by the marketing scheme proposed by the Glendive Chamber
of Commerce. Hence, on 3 March 1989, Governor Stevens signed a bill

making it legal for Glendive's caviar operation to sell paddlefish eggs for the purpose of funding community projects. Included in the legislation was a requirement, happily agreed to by the Glendive chamber, that half the net proceeds from egg sales be returned to the state for paddlefish research and management.

The ink on the new law had barely dried when the chamber of commerce began preparing for the upcoming 1990 spring fishing season. They brought in a Russian caviar expert to help transform an abandoned local dairy into a processing plant, where the eggs could be soaked in brine. Twelve workers were hired to clean fish, and a wholesale distributer was found for the caviar. After several months of preparation, Glendive enviro-capitalists were ready to start turning formerly wasted eggs into profits for the community.

In 1990, its first season of operation, workers cleaned 1,600 paddlefish and processed over 4,000 pounds of roe. Caviar income totaled $110,000. High water made 1991 the program's most lucrative year, with 3,000 paddlefish cleaned and over 10,000 pounds of roe processed. Caviar income totaled $292,905.

Assuming the 1996 estimate of $200,000 holds, the project will have grossed nearly $1,060,000 from caviar sales after seven years of operation (Carlson 1996). Of that amount, the project has given $220,000 in grants to 117 community projects in twelve eastern Montana counties for cultural, historical, and recreational projects and another $260,000 to the Montana Department of Fish, Wildlife, and Parks for paddlefish research and management. Not bad for a small cowboy town in eastern Montana.

The success of Glendive's enviro-capitalists has not gone unnoticed. In 1993, both Harvard University and the Ford Foundation recognized their caviar project as one of the most innovative programs in the United States. That same year, a group of enterprising individuals in North Dakota, the state that shares the Yellowstone River's paddlefish with Montana, decided it would like to emulate the success of Glendive. The Williston Chamber of Commerce and the Friends of Fort Union Trading Post combined efforts to launch Gold Star Caviar, an operation modeled after the Glendive's project. Gold Star provides free fish-cleaning services in return for donations of paddlefish roe and sells the processed roe to a wholesale buyer. A portion of the net proceeds from caviar sales are paid to North Dakota's Game and Fish Department for research, public information on paddlefish, and enforcement of fishing regulations. The remainder goes to nonprofit groups in the Williston area for historical, cultural, and recreational projects. In its first year of operation, Gold Star netted $14,000 from the sale of paddlefish caviar.

Not only do these two projects pay for baseball parks, museums, and libraries in towns strapped for money, they are helping sustain Yellowstone River paddlefish. With half of the profits invested in paddlefish management, state wildlife officials can conduct research to understand the needs of this prehistoric fish, better regulate fishing pressure, and monitor water quality and spawning habitat. The paddlefish entrepreneurs have transformed waste into wealth in more ways than one.

A River Runs By It

Land development in Boise, Idaho, offers an example of how profits from housing can be linked to stream reclamation. In this case, the enviro-capitalist Peter S. O'Neill recognized the growing demand for natural amenities in an urban setting and responded by building communities for people as well as fish. Among his early achievements was a project that revitalized a river and created one of the nation's first urban spawning streams for trout. O'Neill recognized that visually pleasing and biologically productive surroundings are assets that add to property values. Hence, his housing developments offer free-flowing trout streams, lush streamside vegetation, and biologically diverse lakes and wetlands.

Consider one of O'Neill's early projects, a 650-unit residential development in Boise called River Run. Most of the property was originally land heavily grazed by livestock. From the project's beginnings in 1977, O'Neill emphasized enhancing the property's natural amenities to increase the value of homes. A brochure on River Run describes the developer's intentions: "River Run has been designed and built with a sensitivity to the natural environment found here. The plan has always been to create and insure premium value for homeowners and residents" (River Run Development Company N.d.).

Located on the east side of Boise, the development spans 120 acres along the Boise River. River Run's single-family homes, condominiums, and custom homes were built to blend into the natural surroundings of the Boise River. The property's own natural amenities were enhanced by construction of a seven-acre lake called Heron Lake and several free-flowing streams.

But as a partner in the River Run Development Company, O'Neill was not satisfied with these efforts. To him, it was obvious that the development could improve the environment even more, especially where there was an unsightly half-mile flood-relief channel that paralleled the northern border of the development and the Boise River. The channel was designed and built by the Army Corps of Engineers for flood control, not beauty. The straight, cobble-lined channel through which water flowed during high water dried up during low water, and in O'Neill's words "looked like hell." If its water flowed continuously, the channel had the potential to be a beautiful stream.

To transform this ugly flood control channel, O'Neill needed an additional source of water. At the time, River Run's other waterways were receiving about twenty cubic feet per second of water from Loggers Creek, a small tributary of the Boise River. This source was not enough to keep water flowing throughout the summer in both the existing waterways in River Run and the flood control channel. O'Neill estimated he needed ten cubic feet per second from the Boise River to ensure continuous flow in the channel. By his calculations that was less than 6 percent of the existing flow.

The Boise River flows out of the mountains and through the city. It is a clear, cold river that offers a multitude of wildlife habitats along its shores, as well as numerous recreational opportunities for residents. The water quality is good, and the river provides an opportunity to catch rainbow and brown trout within city limits, much to the delight of local fishermen. The only problem with the river was that it lacked natural trout spawning habitat and therefore required annual restocking by the fish and game department to sustain the fishery.

In the fall of 1982, O'Neill applied for a water right to divert the ten cubic feet per second from the Boise River into the flood control channel. Concerned that the diversion might further reduce the stream's spawning potential, however, the Idaho Department of Fish and Game protested the diversion, arguing that it would reduce to below the minimum the streamflow needed to maintain trout populations in the river.

O'Neill, himself an avid trout fisherman, understood the officials' concerns, but believed there was potential to make a substantial improvement. At the suggestion of the state fish and game department, he contacted Timberline Reclamation, Inc. (later renamed Inter-Fluve, Inc.), a Bozeman, Montana, scientific and engineering firm nationally recognized for rehabilitating trout streams. O'Neill's plan was to turn the relief channel into a year-round trout stream complete with spawning habitat. He wanted to show that the additional water provided from the Boise River could both enhance the amenities of River Run and improve the trout fishery.

The problem with the Boise River was that it lacked small gravel beds and clear-flowing, well-oxygenated water necessary for trout spawning habitat. Such spawning beds are usually created as a river's natural flow wears away boulders and gradually moves downstream rocks, pebbles, and other river-bottom particles. This process, however, had been severely limited when the natural flow of the Boise was regulated by Lucky Peak Dam, eight miles upstream from River Run. The spawning beds that existed before the dam was built had long since been washed downstream or been silted over as the dam held back the replacement gravel.

O'Neill hired Timberline to study the feasibility and costs of converting the flood control channel into a trout spawning stream. The study cost O'Neill $15,000, an investment that turned out to be worth every penny. Timberline concluded that with appropriate modifications the channel could easily be turned into a productive stream. The company also recommended modifications to Lake Heron and the other waterways in the River Run development. At a cost of $30,000 for modifying the flood control channel, the investment was substantial, but O'Neill decided to push ahead with the project.

Before he could break any ground, however, he had to overcome regulatory hurdles on several levels. To make the appropriate modifications, O'Neill needed to get approval for the project from the Idaho Department of Water Resources, the Boise Parks Department, the U.S. Bureau of Reclamation, and the U.S. Army Corps of Engineers. Fortunately, after O'Neill presented his new plan for using additional water to create trout habitat, Idaho wildlife officials dropped their objection to the water right application. They became strong supporters of O'Neill's project and eventually helped him get necessary approvals from the other agencies.

The project was carried out in various stages between 1984 and 1989. The flood control channel was reshaped using concrete and log structures to create a meandering flow with pools, riffles, and spawning beds. Similar modifications were made to other streams in the River Run system. Heron Lake was deepened. In addition, over two miles of new streams were created throughout the residential complex. Finally, to help trout from the Boise River enter the River Run system, one fish ladder was constructed at the irrigation gate of Loggers Creek and another at the outflow from Heron Lake.

Because it took several years for vegetation to take hold and spread along the stream banks, the benefits of the project were not immediately visible. But once the natural system began to mature, the amenities became more visible, and the trout began to flourish. According to state biologist Scott Grunder, a 1991 electroshock survey of the channel found many trout. Says Grunder, "It's obvious that trout are thriving in the channel now."[7]

Since completing River Run, O'Neill has developed four other projects and is working on a fifth in McCall, Idaho. Each of the projects has his signature—beautiful natural surroundings and enhanced habitat for fish and wildlife. At the Lane Ranch, a residential project in Sun Valley, Idaho, O'Neill hired Inter-Fluve's team of fish biologists, botanists, and hydrologists to transform Elkhorn Creek, an irrigation ditch for alfalfa fields, into a biologically diverse riparian corridor for fish and wildlife. The team created

> a system of ponds, streams, and wetlands, lined with trees, shrubs, and meadow grasses. In the years to come, as the vegetation matures, this new riparian zone will function as a living area for wildlife and provide shade and stream bank stability for fish. . . . Fish will use this corridor on spawning runs from the Big Wood River, something the irrigation network had blocked.[8]

These efforts have given homeowners on the Lane Ranch a valuable and precious resource that adds to their living pleasure. O'Neill's Spring Meadows development offers another example. There he hired Inter-Fluve to relocate an existing stream to flow within the Spring Meadow residential community and rehabilitate adjacent lands for incorporation into Boise's city park complex. The project also improved wetlands, protected sensitive eagle nesting sites, and created trout habitat. Similar rehabilitation projects were carried out at The Springs development and at Meadow Creek, both in Boise. O'Neill's Spring Mountain Ranch creates "new wetlands, approximately 7.5 acres of ponds, and 6,000 feet of enhanced stream corridors."[9]

Has the expense and trouble been worth it for O'Neill? Undoubtedly, his housing developments command a financial premium because of their amenities. But on a personal level, O'Neill enjoys a tremendous personal satisfaction from the way he improved the environment. Because the River Run project was the first residential development in the country to create viable trout habitat from its waterways, O'Neill's development has been used by the Idaho Department of Fish and Game as an example of what other developers can do to help restore urban rivers. The Urban Land Institute awarded O'Neill the Design Excellence Award for his River Run project.

The Road Ahead

These three examples illustrate how entrepreneurial skills can be successfully used to improve the environment. In each case an enviro-capitalist recognized the possibilities of doing something differently. As a wildlife biologist, Tom Bourland saw that to achieve his wildlife objectives in a commercial forest, he had to make wildlife an asset instead of a liability. Rather than being impeded by the frustration of meeting the bottom line, he used it to the advantage of the resource and the people who enjoy it, as well as the company. Outside capital investment was not necessary, but Bourland did have to convince International Paper's decision makers that their assets could be employed more productively. During the thirty years needed for timber in the Southeast to grow from seedlings to harvestable trees, the company expends a lot to nurture the trees but receives almost no revenues. It was Bourland's implementation of a fee-recreation program that allowed IP to transform this liability into an asset. To do so, the company marketed new products and formed new contracts (some formal and some informal) with customers. The job was complicated by the fact that neither the buyer nor seller was familiar with this market. Bourland the biologist had to become Bourland the salesman. He had to convince hunters that paying for hunting and participating in game management was worth the price. He had to devise contracts that made clear what the company would provide and what the hunters would pay in return. In short, he applied standard business marketing and management skills in a new way, the essence of entrepreneurship.

But it is not always profit that drives enviro-capitalists, as the "cowboy caviar" example shows. The civic leaders of Glendive were confronted with the problem faced by so many small towns across the nation: where can they get the money for Little League, youth camps, parks, and art projects? Frank Crisafulli, a successful entrepreneur in the sprinkler irrigation business, recognized the potential for linking profits from marketing paddlefish caviar with community spirit. Because most people who spend hours trying to snag a paddlefish have no interest in the roe, they are willing to donate them, especially when they know the profits will go to enhancing the fishery and the community. Again, little capital was required, but marketing and management skills were crucial. Especially important was convincing state and federal wildlife officials that changing the law was a good idea because those officials were not generally enamored with marketing wildlife. This sales job was perhaps the biggest challenge faced by the Montana enviro-capitalists. Once the law was changed, they contracted with these same officials to share the profits for paddlefish research, a way to make the marketing of caviar a win-win solution for all.

Building houses always requires capital, but raising that capital under normal circumstances was not a problem for Peter O'Neill because he had a good product. However, he faced a new situation when he recognized that the growing market for environmental amenities could be packaged with his housing development to enhance profits and fish habitat. Because this development project cost a little more, he had to convince investors that there was a market for the product and that people would pay high enough prices for the houses to cover the costs. The contracting problem O'Neill faced was one of being able to collect money from the people who would enjoy the amenity. Often, these people expect and get a free lunch from public and private landowners whose lands provide wildlife habitat. By combining a larger block of land with the potential trout habitat, O'Neill was able to capture the amenity values in the housing price. The success of his entrepreneurial efforts is demonstrated by his expansion and by other projects copying his approach.

Entrepreneurial approaches that capitalize on profits in the marketplace offer an important alternative for producing environmental quality in a world where acrimony and tight budgets dominate most policy debates. By harnessing consumer demands for products related to the environment and by contracting with input owners to meet those demands, enviro-capitalists can supplement the standard regulatory approach.

In the following chapters, we visit other enviro-capitalists at work, illustrating their discovery that markets and environmental quality can mix. We begin with a trip back in time to challenge the notion that only a few "unselfish" conservationists recognized environmental values in the late nineteenth century. To the contrary, some of the same robber barons who dominate the history of railroading, ranching, and logging were also "barons of preservation," recognizing that profits could be made from preserving environmental amenities (chapter 2). "Mavericks of conservation" defied the standard environmental stereotype that only government can protect amenities and were spurred by a

desire to preserve them through the use of markets and private ownership (chapter 3). Market hunters in the early twentieth century drove
some species to extinction or near extinction because they only owned
dead animals. Today, enviro-capitalists like Tom Bourland are finding
ways to profit from owning habitat. Engaging in the "business of
Bambi" (chapter 4), these entrepreneurs see markets as a tool to turn
wildlife into assets and profits into more wildlife. "Buy that fish a
drink" is the way aquatic entrepreneurs such as Zach Willey and Andrew Purkey are moving water from irrigation back into streams, thus
restoring fish habitat (chapter 5). A growing demand to live with nature while retaining all the comforts of home created a niche in the
housing market, especially in the West. Following the lead of Peter
O'Neill, "eco-developers"are filling that niche (chapter 6). Enviro-capitalists are not just found in the United States. For example, enviro-
capitalist Orri Vigfusson, who is helping the recovery of Atlantic
salmon sport fisheries, joins a growing list of entrepreneurs who are
"going global" (chapter 7). As we saw with the little town of Glendive,
not all enviro-capitalists work in corporations. From the Fort Apache
Indian Reservation in Arizona to native communal lands in Zimbabwe,
the "community spirit" for environmental amenities is alive and well
(chapter 8). Unfortunately, enviro-capitalists can be frustrated by bureaucratic constraints. Moreover, bureaucrats charged with enhancing
the environment often lack incentives to be entrepreneurs. "The good,
the bad, and the ugly" sides of our current political and legal institutions (chapter 9) illustrate how we might get the right incentives in the
political sector for enviro-capitalists to flourish.

Notes

1. For an excellent discussion of the politics of the elephant issue and the
negative incentives it has generated, see Bonner (1993).

2. For a discussion of this awakening to wildlife values, see Bourland (1986).

3. For details, see Killian (1991, 78–79).

4. Telephone interview with Michael Carlson, President, Glendive Chamber
of Commerce, 6 August 1992.

5. This is the same reason put forth for banning trade in other animal products such as ivory under the CITES treaty.

6. Letter from K. L. Cool, Director, Montana Department of Fish, Wildlife,
and Parks, to Joel Medlin, U.S. Fish and Wildlife Service, 8 June 1990.

7. Interview with Scott Grunder, environmental staff biologist, Idaho Fish
and Game Department, 29 June 1994.

8. Data on Lane Ranch provided by O'Neill Enterprises, Inc., Boise, Idaho.

9. Data on Spring Mountain Ranch provided by O'Neill Enterprises, Inc., Boise, Idaho.

References

Bonner, Raymond. 1993. *At the Hand of Man: Peril and Hope for Africa's Wildlife.* New York: Knopf.

Bourland, Tom. 1986. Social Trends and Market Influences Affecting an Industrial Wildlife Program. Presentation at Game Bird Seminar, Albany, GA, sponsored by Tall Timbers Association, fall.

————. 1988. International Paper's Wildlife Management and Public Recreation Programs. Presentation at Seminar for Congressional Staff Members, Big Sky, MT, sponsored by the Political Economy Research Center, December 7–11.

Carlson, Michael. 1996. Report on Glendive Paddlefish Program. Presentation given at a regional conference for journalists, Monticello, MN, sponsored by the Political Economy Research Center, July 11–14.

Hughes, Jonathan R. T. 1986. *The Vital Few: The Entrepreneur and American Economic Progress.* Oxford, England: Oxford University Press.

Killian, Linda. 1991. A Walk in the Woods. *Forbes*, September 30.

River Run Development Company. N.d. *River Run: The Program for Improving Trout Habitat.* Boise, ID: River Run Development Company.

Schulz, Bill. 1992. Caviar Cravers Land Paddlefish in Hot Water. *Great Falls Tribune*, July 2.

Starnes, Richard. 1982. Timber Wakes Up. *Outdoor Life*, January.

Chapter 2

Barons of Preservation

What recommends commerce to me is its enterprise and bravery.
It does not clasp its hands and pray to Jupiter.

—Henry David Thoreau

Robber barons. The name says it all. These entrepreneurs of the late nineteenth century allegedly robbed the public of their money and their natural resources. Timber, oil, railroad, and mining executives who operated the companies that dominate the history of the American frontier are portrayed as profitmongers interested in acquiring wealth as fast as possible without any concern for either people or the environment. As history generally portrays them, these men lacked the vision and soul for preserving our natural heritage. Had the robber barons been left to their own devices without governmental regulation and control of lands, places like Yellowstone National Park would have been laid to waste. Saving such places required a few unselfish visionaries who revered the grandeur of nature and recognized the value of preserving natural resources not for the sake of profits but for future generations. As historian John Ise (1961, 1) said of our national parks, "We have this great system of national parks, monuments, and other areas not as a result of public demand but because a few farsighted, unselfish, and idealistic men and women foresaw the national need and got the areas established and protected in one way or another, fighting public inertia and selfish commercial interests."

Economists have contributed to the view that protecting amenities and seeking profits do not mix by arguing, in theory, at least, that profit seekers are too shortsighted to consider the long-term benefits of preservation or that they cannot capture the value of amenities in their bottom line. Capturing this may be especially difficult if the resource will continue to create value for future generations. For exam-

21

ple, Sterling Brubaker (1983, 103) of Resources for the Future, one of the nation's leading resource think tanks, says, "Securing the interests of future generations (beyond one or two) is a social and not a private concern." He argues that public intervention is necessary because "private individuals lack the power or incentive to do it."

Certainly, natural resources were used more extensively in the nineteenth century, and preservation did not receive the same emphasis that it does today. However, before dismissing a positive role for profit seekers in amenity protection, we must ask whether they did not take on the task because of market failure or because of differences in scarcity then and now. Debates over resource scarcity are endless, but substantial evidence suggests that in the nineteenth century, most natural resources were abundant and were not becoming more scarce.[1] In this setting, preservation made little sense for either private entrepreneurs or politicians trying to do good. Moreover, throughout most of the nineteenth century, virtually everyone viewed wilderness as an area to be tamed to support the safe expansion of human habitat. It was not until the late nineteenth century that people with free time, wealth, and transportation began seeking wilderness experiences. Only at that point would we expect to see entrepreneurial radars locking onto the provision of environmental amenities. Indeed, this is what happened.

All Aboard the Yellowstone Express

Because Yellowstone National Park was created by the federal government more than a century ago, many people assume that the park must have been established because a "few farsighted, unselfish, and idealistic men and women foresaw the national need and got the areas established and protected." On the contrary, it was profit-seeking envirocapitalists who recognized the amenity values of preservation and tried to capture them.[2]

John Colter was the first white man to explore the upper Yellowstone Basin in the fall of 1807. Because of his unbelievable descriptions of geysers spewing steam and canyons cutting deep into the earth, the region was branded "Colter's Hell." In 1834 Warren Angus Fergus became the first real tourist to visit the region. Fascinated rather than frightened by the descriptions of trappers, he made the trip with two Indians and reported in great detail the wonders of geysers, mud pots, and thermal springs. The famous trapper Osborne Russell made the first of five trips to the upper Yellowstone region in 1835, and stated afterward, "There is something in the wild romantic scenery of this valley which I cannot . . . describe. . . . For my own part I almost wished I could spend the remainder of many days in a place like this where happiness and contentment seemed to reign in wild romantic splendor" (quoted in Haines 1977, 1:49).

In the early 1860s, prospectors followed the fur traders and trappers. Individuals and groups searching for gold carried out numerous explorations, but except for some relatively small strikes in the vicinity of present-day Cooke City, at the northeast corner of the park, little was found. Nevertheless the prospectors added to the growing knowledge of the region's special features and to its reputation as a unique place worth visiting.

The reputation of the region grew and finally culminated with three more formal expeditions to map and explore the area in 1869, 1870, and 1871. The first consisted of three Helena, Montana, residents, David Folsom, Charles Cook, and William Peterson, who left Helena with five horses in early September and returned five weeks later. They visited Tower Falls, saw the Grand Canyon of the Yellowstone, the upper and lower falls, and spent time in the thermal areas. A summary of their trip published in the *Western Monthly Magazine*, July 1871, further increased public awareness of the "wonderland."

In 1870 an expedition led by Henry D. Washburn, the newly appointed surveyor-general of Montana, explored the Yellowstone area from 17 August through 27 September. Several important business and political leaders of the Montana Territory accompanied the expedition, including Nathaniel P. Langford, who later became the first superintendent of Yellowstone Park. Much publicity came from this expedition, as several members gave lectures about their experiences, and magazines and newspapers published stories about the wonders of the area.

Finally, in 1871 Dr. Ferdinand Vandiveer Hayden, head of the U.S. Geological and Geographical Survey in the territories, petitioned Congress to fund an official exploration of the region. Congress appropriated $40,000 for the expedition, excluding the Army's costs of providing mounts and equipment. The Union Pacific Railway provided free transportation for survey personnel to Ogden, Utah. Hayden's party consisted of twenty-one men, including photographer William Henry Jackson and artist Thomas Moran.

After Hayden's survey was completed in the fall of 1871, and he returned to Washington, D.C., events unfolded rapidly in the nation's capital. A bill to create the first national park was introduced on 18 December 1871, passed both houses with little opposition, and was signed into law by President Grant on 1 March 1872.

Several individuals claimed credit for the idea of creating a national park in the Yellowstone area. The traditional story as recounted from Nathaniel P. Langford's diary is that members of the 1870 expedition came up with the idea while sitting around the campfire (Haines 1977, 1:129–30). There is some doubt, however, whether this discussion actually occurred because Langford did not edit and publish his diary until 1905, thirty-five years after the campfire in question.

> There is . . . no mention of the term "national park" in any of the numerous publications prepared by the members of the Washburn Expedition following their exploits; the omission is very surprising in light of the plan's supposed adoption by all but one of the explorers. Thus it is reasonable to conclude that while Langford did not intentionally distort his recollections, they magnified over time in response to the growing popularity of the national park idea. (Runte 1979, 42)

Several other individuals claimed credit for the idea of making the area into a government reserve. Montana's territorial delegate William Clagett, who introduced the bill into the Congress, said twenty years later, "so far as my personal knowledge goes, the first idea of making it a public park occurred to myself" (quoted in Bartlett 1974, 198). Ferdinand V. Hayden also claimed that "So far as I know, I originated the idea of the park. . ." (quoted in Bartlett 1974, 201). General Phillip H. Sheridan took credit because he sent the Barlow-Heap expedition to the region in 1871, the same year as the Hayden expedition. William Henry Jackson believed his photographs, widely distributed in the Congress prior to the passage of the legislation, made the difference. Though the precise origin of the idea of preserving the amenity values in the Yellowstone region as a national park is not known, it is clear that these values were recognized almost immediately.

This recognition suggests that there might have been competition by private entrepreneurs to capture the value inherent in Yellowstone's natural wonders. Indeed, by 1870 two profit seekers were cutting poles to fence off the geyser basins, and in 1871 two others preempted 320 acres that covered Mammoth Hot Springs (see Jackson 1957). Another entrepreneur, C. J. Baronett, tried to capture a share of the profits by building and maintaining a toll bridge across the Yellowstone River just above its junction with the Lamar River during the summer of 1871 (Jackson 1957, 56). And finally, "Yankee Jim" and his partners Bart Henderson and Horn Miller built a toll road through a narrow cut, now Yankee Jim Canyon, along the Yellowstone River north of Yellowstone. Yankee Jim squatted on the land he needed to construct the road in 1871, twelve years before the land was surveyed, and opened his National Park Toll Road in July 1873. Unfortunately sufficient records do not remain to determine whether the toll bridge or toll road generated large profits, but that Baronett contemplated building a second bridge across the Lamar River, after the government purchased his first bridge, suggests that there must have been some profits in the venture.[3]

These piecemeal efforts, however, were insignificant compared to the efforts of the most active private interest in the region, the Northern Pacific Railroad, chartered by Congress on 2 July 1862. Josiah Perham, the entrepreneur responsible for its founding, originally planned to take the railroad across the center of the nation but the Union Pacific and Central Pacific beat him to that route. He therefore moved his route to the north. In 1869 Jay Cooke and Company joined in financing the venture, obtaining a majority interest and operating control of the company. Interestingly, the northeast gateway to the park, Cooke City, was named for the financier because he promised to build a railroad through Yellowstone to the gateway.

Because Cooke planned to raise a considerable portion of his capital by the sale of bonds, profitable passenger operations were important. Given Yellowstone's distance from population centers, the railroad was in a good position to capitalize on the amenity value of the park.

> Vacationers in those days did not lightheartedly pack a sandwich and a thermos of coffee and mount saddle horses or drive buggies to resorts, spas, or playgrounds for an afternoon's recreation. Four-footed transport would have taken the entire summer for a visit. Trains covered the distance faster, carrying fare-paying people who contributed a steady revenue to the railroad coffers. (Peterson 1985, 20)

Recognizing the potential for carrying passengers to Yellowstone, Cooke invited Nathaniel Langford to his Philadelphia estate on 4 and 5 July 1870. Upon returning home to Montana, Langford provided the leadership for the Washburn expedition in 1870. As noted above, Langford accompanied the expedition, assembling information suitable for publicity purposes (see Haines 1977, 2:137). After the group returned, he spent six weeks putting 35,000 words of notes into manuscripts suitable for publication. Langford went on tour of the East under contract to Cooke and gave twenty lectures promoting the region, including one in Washington, D.C., attended by several members of Congress. He also delivered a private address to Cooke and his friends at Cooke's Philadelphia estate on 26 May 1871. In several articles published in the popular press and in speeches about Yellowstone, Langford was careful to point out the importance of the Northern Pacific as a means of transportation to the region (Runte 1990, 6).

Later, the railroad solicited Hayden to lobby on behalf of the legislation to establish the national park. In addition to seeking support from Langford and Hayden, the Northern Pacific took advantage of the talents of noted landscape painter Thomas Moran. The railroad provided the necessary financing for Moran, who accompanied the Hayden expedition in 1871.

There is little doubt from their early investments that the owners of the railroad recognized the unique features of Yellowstone from the outset and that, because they provided the only major transportation for tourists, they were in an enviable position of capturing most of the tourist dollars. Historian Alfred Runte (1979, 45) notes that "Cooke and his associates realized, of course, that if Yellowstone became a park, their railroad would be sole beneficiary of the tourist traffic."

The only question was how they would prevent the potential rewards from being captured by small developers like those who had begun fencing the geyser basins and hot springs and building toll roads and bridges. Private ownership of Yellowstone by the railroad might have been the most secure way of capturing the amenity values, but the land laws at the time worked against such an approach. The Homestead Act of 1862 required that land be farmed, and other lands laws required mining and logging to establish private ownership. All of these requirements would have reduced the values that the railroad thought important, and none of the laws provided for establishing ownership of amenities. Moreover, the acreage limitations for each claim (initially 160 but eventually 640 acres) worked against the railroad's ownership of a sufficiently large area to capture the tourist dollars and in favor of small areas owned by several individuals.

For the railroad with a virtual monopoly on transportation to the region, the best alternative was to preserve the region intact as a scenic national park. In a letter to Hayden dated 27 October 1871, Jay Cooke's publicity man states that Congress should "pass a bill reserving the Great Geyser Basin as a public park forever—just as it has reserved that far inferior wonder the Yosemite Valley and the big trees. If you approve this, would such a recommendation be appropriate in your final report?" (quoted in Bartlett 1974, 206–7). This proposal came from Judge William Darrah Kelley, a Republican congressman from Pennsylvania and business associate of Cooke. Just three days after the letter was written, Cooke wrote to W. Milner Roberts, his aide in Montana:

We are delighted to hear such good accounts of the Yellowstone expedition from both ends. Gen. Hancock and Gen. Sheridan have both telegraphed that the report will be a splendid one from the expedition at this end. . . . It is proposed by Mr. Hayden in his report to Congress that the Geyser region around Yellowstone Lake shall be set apart by government as park, similar to that of the Great Trees & other reservations in California. Would this conflict with our land grant, or interfere with us in any way? Please give me your views on this subject. It is important to do something speedily, or squatters and claimants will go in there, and we can probably deal much better with the government in any improvements we may desire to make for the benefit of our pleasure travel than with individuals. (quoted in Bartlett 1974, 208)

W. Milner Roberts responded by telegram from Helena, on 21 November 1871: "Your October thirtieth and November sixth rec'd. Geysers outside our grant advise Congressional delegation be in East probably before middle December" (quoted in Bartlett 1974, 208). The Northern Pacific's interest in preserving the amenity values in Yellowstone is clear from the statement from a representative of the company:

We do not want to see the Falls of the Yellowstone driving the looms of a cotton factory, or the great geysers boiling pork for some gigantic packing house, but in all the native majesty and grandeur in which they appear today, without, as yet, a single trace of that adornment which is desecration, that improvement which is equivalent to ruin, or that utilization which means utter destruction. (quoted in Runte 1990, 23)

Thus, the officials of the Northern Pacific recognized the value of Yellowstone and were able to capture most of the tourist dollars by supporting the creation of a national park. Their efforts on behalf of the park were immediately successful. In his official report, Hayden did include the suggestion that the area be set aside as a government preserve; Langford was in Washington throughout the debate on the park legislation to lobby for passage; a collection of Jackson's photographs was placed on the desk of every member of Congress; and some of Moran's watercolors were distributed to influential senators and representatives (Bartlett 1974, 208). It is little wonder that the bill passed quickly with only token opposition.

Similarly, the profit motive for railroads emerged in the establishment of other early national parks in the nineteenth century. Railroad interest lay behind nearly all of the major western national parks established in this era: Glacier National Park and the Great Northern Railroad; Mount Rainier National Park and the Tacoma Eastern Railroad; Crater Lake and the Southern Pacific Railroad; and Grand Canyon National Park and the Santa Fe Railway (Schwantes 1993, 209–12). Behind each was an enviro-capitalist who recognized value in the natural environment and saw potential to capture it by providing transportation and tourist services. They were profit motivated, but their actions resulted in the preservation of cornerstones in our national park system.

Cowboy Entrepreneurs

Beyond the railroads' efforts to capture western amenities, dude ranchers capitalized on the desires of turn-of-the-century easterners who wanted to experience life in the Old West. These would-be cowboys wanted a place where they could ride horses, rope cattle, sleep under the stars, fish, and hunt. These were the "amenities" provided by early dude ranch entrepreneurs.

> Whether they were native Westerners who had started as cattle and horse ranchers, or eastern "dudes" who returned to the West to live forever the life they had first experienced as guests on someone else's ranch, they brought with them their own unique interests, attitudes, and background. As they developed their holdings, each ranch began to reflect the special personality of its owners. The dudes came to recognize these differences and selected their "own" ranch accordingly. (Bernstein 1982, 15)

Alden, Willis, and Howard Eaton, brothers from Pittsburgh, Pennsylvania, were among the first dude ranching entrepreneurs. After many treks west, Howard, the eldest, headed for the Dakota Badlands to start a cattle ranch, and his brothers soon followed. The spread they acquired by squatter's rights became known as the Custer Trail Ranch. In addition to being a successful cattle and horse operation in the late 1870s, the ranch was a place for the Eatons' friends from the East to enjoy ranch life. As their guest list grew beyond their immediate circle of friends, they began charging for the services of the ranch. In 1879, the Eatons moved their cattle and dude ranching operation to the Big Horn Mountains in Wyoming because the setting provided more scenery and opportunities for recreation. The new 7,000-acre ranch provided everything an outdoor enthusiast could want; clear, cold, trout streams for fishermen, deer and elk for hunters, forested mountains for hikers, and open range for "ranch-work" enthusiasts. Today, the ranch still operates as a combined working cattle ranch and dude ranch.

Others were also capitalizing on the market for ranch life and preserving the associated amenity values. Abner E. Sprague, for example, started a combined cattle and guest ranch in scenic Moraine Park, Colorado that operated until 1962. At that time, the amenity values were considered important enough to be purchased by the National Park Service for $750,000.

Windham Thomas Wyndam-Quinn, better known as the Earl of Dunraven, was another entrepreneur who decided to market the ranching experience. The adventuresome earl settled near Estes Park, Colorado, for the purpose of establishing a cattle operation. "Herbage was plentiful, and cattle could feed all winter, for the snow never lay. It was an ideal cattle-ranch, and to that purpose we put it" (Earl of Dunraven 1922, 142).

To preserve enough land for his operation, the earl had to overcome the 160-acre limitation of the Homestead Act. To do so, he had Estes Park legally surveyed and then contracted with local townspeople to file claims on 160-acre parcels and resell them to him for an estimated price of $5 per acre. From 1874 to 1880, the earl acquired 8,200 acres of land. His efforts to acquire the entire 20,000 acres of Estes Park were eventually stymied, however, by other entrepreneurs who wanted to capitalize on the dude ranching potential of the area.

The Earl of Dunraven also realized the recreational potential of the park: "The air is scented with the sweet-smelling sap of the pines, whose branches welcome many feathered visitors from southern climes; an occasional hummingbird whirrs among the shrubs, trout leap in the creeks, insects buzz in the air; all nature is active and exuberant with life" (Earl of Dunraven 1914, 36). To meet the growing demand from the "eastern tourist," the earl built a lodge on his ranch and began catering to guests in 1877. With elk hunting and trout fishing, plus cattle ranching, the earl's property offered guests a grand spectacle of the American West. He eventually sold the operation to Freelan O. Stanley, coinventor of the Stanley Steamer, who opened the Stanley Hotel on the property in 1909.

The ability of these enviro-capitalists to recognize and capture the scenic and recreational values is evidenced by the fact that their lands were targeted by the National Park Service for inclusion in Rocky Mountain National Park. In 1974, for example, John Holzwarth's Trout Lodge, which opened in 1920, was purchased by the Nature Conservancy and then transferred to the National Park Service (Kaye 1983).

Most of the dude ranching properties in this region were purchased in the 1950s and 1960s by the Park Service as additions to Rocky Mountain National Park. The Park Service removed many of the historic buildings so that the area could be returned to more "natural conditions." Not everyone, however, was enamored with their removal, "especially as they were replaced by new automobile campgrounds" (Buccholtz 1983, 205). "We can't quite understand why folks who desire lodge accommodations are denied the same privilege of 'living in the park,'" opined the local newspaper, the *Estes Park Trail*, on 18 October 1957. "A hundred people living at a lodge create less confusion, less muss and fuss, than a hundred camping out." In removing the historic buildings, the National Park Service has lost a part of the cowboy culture, but at least much of the natural environment preserved by the dude ranching entrepreneurs remains intact.

A Forest Retreat

Just as the influence of the iron, copper, and lumber booms was fading in the Great Lake states, Americans in the Upper Midwest and Northeast were retreating to the woods for their summer vacations. Entrepreneurs in northern Michigan responded by creating hunting and fishing camps and land clubs that provided the opportunities and facilities that vacationing visitors sought. The process preserved a very extraordinary place.

In the middle of the nineteenth century, Michigan's Upper Peninsula was a mecca for loggers and miners. In 1862 over 100,000 tons of ore passed through the Sault Ste. Marie Canal that linked Lakes Superior and Huron, and the next year, that amount almost tripled. Lumberjacks also were scouring Michigan's lower peninsula searching for an alternative to New England's sagging timber production. When timber supplies in the lower peninsula dwindled, those loggers moved to the Upper Peninsula.[4]

As virgin forests became scarcer in the 1880s, recreationists from the industrialized centers of the Upper Midwest and Northeast were discovering the beauty of the Huron Mountain region, located near the mouth of the Pine River on the Lake Superior side of the Upper Peninsula. Historian Archer Mayor writes,

> Cheek by jowl with lumbermen and the miners, summer vacationers were crowding the Superior coast, seeking to escape the hurly-burly of their

prosperous lives. And they were not just from Michigan, but from all over the greater industrial Northeast. The Upper Peninsula, like the Adirondack Mountains in New York, offered the serenity of woods and lakes and fish-filled streams, even among the tumultuous rumbling of a countryside in full flux. (Mayor 1988, 3)

It was a virtual paradise for those who enjoyed the outdoors. In the words of one visiting sportsman from Pittsburgh, "Game was abundant—deer, wild pigeons, and grouse. Pigeons fed in great numbers on the huckleberries in the woods between the mouth of the river and Pine Lake. The forest was practically untouched. Bears were few. Wolves made a great noise at night, and their tracks were plentiful" (quoted in Mayor 1988, 5).

The lure of the countryside and importance of preserving its recreational potential was not overlooked by one entrepreneur in the region, Horatio Seymour Jr. The Marquette-based manager of the Michigan Land & Iron Company came up with the idea of forming a 100-member hunting and fishing land club to purchase land in the Huron Mountain area. In 1887, he approached his friend John M. Longyear, a prosperous land dealer, with the idea. Longyear initially rejected Seymour's idea, believing that the area was too remote and rugged to draw tourists. He did allow, however, that he would join Seymour in the venture if Seymour could interest other prominent people.

When Seymour approached Longyear again in 1889, he had a much stronger case for a land club in the Huron Mountain area. Seymour had found prominent individuals from both Detroit and Marquette willing to become club members. In addition, hunting and fishing camps and land clubs were springing up "like flowers" along the Lake Superior coast near Sault Ste. Marie, and they were spreading west toward the Huron area. No doubt Longyear's enthusiasm was enhanced by his ownership of the steamboat company that provided exclusive service to the area from the lower peninsula and his ownership of several parcels of land near what would be the club's boundaries. Needless to say, he joined Seymour and the others in the venture.

The club, initially called the Huron Mountain Shooting and Fishing Club and later renamed the Huron Mountain Club, was born on 29 November 1897. A twelve-member board was established to oversee club business, and Longyear was appointed the club's first president. Capital for day-to-day operations, the building of a clubhouse, and land acquisition was generated from the sale of member shares and annual dues, priced initially at $100 and $25, respectively. The club began with a fifty-member limit, $5,000 capital, and 7,000 acres acquired through purchase and lease (Mayor 1988, 4).

The club's initial emphasis was on enhancing hunting and fishing opportunities and on improving facilities for hunters and anglers. Additional staff was hired, and a workshop, bathhouses, and boathouses were built on the property. Club employees constructed hiking trails and even built several fish hatcheries to ensure that its lakes and streams had ample supplies of fish. To create a community atmosphere and a stronger incentive to stay with the club through the years, the board ruled that club members could build cabins on the property, leasing sites from the club for $1 per year.

Consistent with the founding goals of the club, the board slowed the pace of investments in improvements and shifted land management emphasis from hunting and fishing toward preservation. For example, in 1897, the club filed a temporary injunction forbidding upstream loggers from running logs down a river that ran adjacent to club property. The outcome was a compromise under which logs could not float down river during the summer (Mayor 1988, 19). When the club's board periodically decided to cut timber to raise capital for improvements or land acquisition, it did so selectively in the exterior region of the property. They always left untouched the interior of the property or "reserved area" (5,000–6,000 acres).

In 1937, the club decided to go a step further in its effort to protect the property's natural amenities. They enlisted the services of Aldo Leopold, the nationally renowned conservationist, to assess the natural and scientific values of the club's holdings and recommend ways to protect them. He found an extraordinary array of both flora and fauna, including white-tailed deer, ruffed grouse, timber wolves, snowshoe rabbits, otters, and an assortment of birds, including spruce hens, pileated woodpeckers, bald eagles, duckhawks, and chimney swifts. Most notably, however, he found a rare and valuable climax forest of maple-hemlock in the club's reserved area. In fact, Leopold concluded, in 1938, that "the Huron Mountain property would soon be one of the few large remnants of maple-hemlock forest remaining in a substantially undisturbed condition." He continued, saying that the club had "not only a unique property, but a large opportunity for public service in science and conservation" (Leopold 1938, 40).

Leopold encouraged the club to continue its land acquisition program by consolidating holdings and creating an additional buffer zone. He recommended that the club preserve habitat for both predator and prey species, an important recommendation at the time given the great division in wildlife circles concerning the importance of predators. Indeed, government bounties on predators had been the order of the day, because predators killed livestock and reduced game species. Finally, Leopold encouraged the club to invite members of the scientific community to pursue their studies on its property.

Since Leopold's Huron Mountain 1938 assessment, the club has continued to follow the policies he recommended without experiencing the political gridlock that often hampers public land management. With little fanfare, the club protected its rare climax forest of maple-hemlock. Moreover, it has served as an important study area for researchers. As we shall see in chapter 6, the legacy of these enviro-capitalists lives on in a modern "eco-developer."

Hugh Macrae's Vision

In the Southeast, a young mining engineer's vision for preserving and capturing the scenic value of a North Carolina mountain provides another example of enviro-capitalism. Hugh Macrae graduated from Massachusetts Institute of Technology in 1885 and embarked on a career as a mining engineer in his home state of North Carolina. As he traveled on horseback to his job in Avery County, he was overwhelmed by the spectacular high country of Grandfather Mountain and its neighboring mountains, Sugar, Grandmother, and Flattop. At 5,964 feet above sea level, Grandfather Mountain's Calloway Peak is actually the highest point in the Blue Ridge Mountains. From there, the view offers a breathtaking panorama stretching across miles of neighboring ridge-tops and valleys. Inspired by the sight, Macrae wrote to his father, Donald Macrae, in Wilmington, Delaware, requesting funds to purchase Grandfather Mountain and sections of the neighboring peaks. Between 1885 and 1890, he purchased a total of 15,750 acres from Walter Waighstill Lenoir.

Young Macrae was interested in buying the mountain so that he could market its natural beauty and vista to visitors. He recognized Grandfather Mountain as a unique asset that could serve as a major tourist attraction for hikers and nature lovers. Like Yellowstone, the mountain was remote, and visitors needed transportation services to the site and tourist facilities once they arrived. Macrae provided both. He built the Yonalossee Road from Linville across the eastern slope of Grandfather Mountain to Blowing Rock, North Carolina, and founded a stagecoach line across the twenty-mile scenic route that today is

Highway 221. To meet the demand for facilities, Macrae developed the resort community of Linville at the base of the mountain in 1889. Linville became one of the smaller stations on the Eastern Tennessee and Western North Carolina Railroad, a line endearingly referred to as "Tweetsie" for the shrill whistle of the railroad's narrow-gauge steam engines. Those engines still operate at another travel attraction between Boone and Blowing Rock, taking visitors back to a time of leisurely, rhythmic travel through the Blue Ridge wilderness.

Macrae's descendants carried on his dreams for Grandfather Mountain. To allow automobiles up Grandfather, Donald, his son, and Julian Morton, husband of his niece Agnes Macrae Morton, widened a horseback trail up the mountain's slope not quite to the top. Though rough, the one-lane road was passable for automobile travel. At the end of the road, the partners constructed a lookout site and charged a toll for using the road and enjoying the spectacular view. When Hugh Morton, Julian's son, took the reins of stewardship for Grandfather Mountain, he wanted to complete the road to the top. Family stockholders stopped the project, questioning his premise that more people would pay to see the view from the top of the mountain, but he still succeeded in widening the existing road and improving the quality of access.

During his control, Hugh Morton fought vigorously to protect the amenity values of the mountain. The main threat came from the federal government's proposed scenic highway, supported by President Franklin D. Roosevelt as a way to stimulate jobs in the isolated Appalachian region. The highway, known as the Blue Ridge Parkway and under control of the National Park Service, was eventually built, but not without a fight from Julian Morton.

In 1939 Donald Macrae and Julian Morton sold the state of North Carolina a right-of-way 1,000 feet wide and eight miles long running across the eastern slope of Grandfather Mountain. In their minds, that right-of-way would not destroy the mountain's aesthetic qualities. But by 1945, plans for the parkway had changed, and engineers were seeking a larger right-of-way that extended higher up the mountain. Hugh Morton refused. At the time, the common engineering practice for crossing rugged mountains was "cut and fill," and Morton felt that this would destroy the "wilderness characteristics" of Grandfather Mountain. The state responded by exercising its right of eminent domain and condemning the parcel.

Morton went before the governor and the highway commission, claiming "abuse of discretion." His lawyers pointed out that the statute that gave the state authority to acquire the land described a "reasonable right-of-way" as 125 acres per mile. Because Donald Macrae and Julian Morton had already sold the state a right-of-way of that size in 1939, Morton argued that condemning any more land violated the law. The governor and the highway commission agreed, and Morton retained the land.

Federal road planners, however, still wanted the higher route, even if it threatened the integrity of the pristine mountainside. The conflict gained public attention in the 1950s and eventually led to a televised debate between Morton and Conrad Worth, head of the National Park Service. Each man was allowed a debate partner, and for his, Morton chose his friend and local television celebrity, Arthur Smith. Morton's comment that to tear up the mountain at the higher elevation would be like "taking a switch blade to the Mona Lisa,"[5] made headlines across the state. Smith followed his friend's emotional appeal by saying that a man who loves his land as Morton loves Grandfather Mountain should not have to fear losing it to "a bunch of Washington bureaucrats." Public opinion had been swayed, and again Morton retained his land.

Today, under an arrangement with the Nature Conservancy, Grandfather Mountain has been permanently protected and remains in private hands. In addition to scenic vistas, the mountain offers a variety of wildlife habitats for species such as bald eagles, black bear, mountain lion, and white-tailed deer. Because of its biological importance, the mountain was designated as an international biosphere reserve by the United Nations.

It is an area in high demand by hikers. As one of the most rugged mountains in the East, Grandfather Mountain has a dozen miles of well-maintained hiking trails, ranging in difficulty from novice to expert. Grandfather Mountain's newly built nature museum houses outstanding exhibits, including interpretations of the natural heritage of the mountain, the finest collection of North Carolina gemstones, minerals and gold, and exhibits of wildflowers. Indian and pioneer history are explored in displays designed by the former chief of natural history exhibits of the Smithsonian Institution.

The Morton family continues its successful marketing of Grandfather Mountain's amenities. Daily fees for all facilities are $9 for adults, $5 for children, and free for children under four. Hiking-only permits are also available at $4.50 for adults and $2.50 for children. Though small in comparison to the federal wilderness system, Grandfather Mountain distinguishes itself as one of the most popular fee-based, private "wilderness areas" in the East.

The Grass Isn't Always Greener

In the bustling port and logging city of Seattle, Washington, we find another case where turn-of-the-century entrepreneurs were preserving their little corner of the world by capitalizing on conservation opportunities. Unlike the previous cases, however, this one has a sad but instructive lesson: the grass is not always greener on the public sector side of the fence.[6]

In 1904, you could hitch a ride on a street car from downtown Seattle to the outskirts of the city and step into Ravenna Park, a pristine forest of Douglas fir trees. While loggers were busy cutting the timber for which the area was famous, these special trees were preserved in the park. Trees there grew as thick as twenty feet in diameter and as tall as four hundred feet. The park quite literally was an urban oasis for nature lovers.

At the time, Ravenna Park was not a national park or even a state or local park. It was privately owned by Mr. and Mrs. W. W. Beck. For the Becks, Ravenna Park's beauty provided both a sense of pride in ownership and a source of income. These enviro-capitalists created Ravenna Park in 1887 by piecing together several parcels of land. The Becks measured and fenced the trees. They even named the more magnificent specimens. To further entice visitors, the Becks built a pavilion for concerts and nature lectures and added paths, benches, and totem poles depicting Northwest Indian culture.

Ravenna Park quickly became immensely popular. Visitors paid 25 cents a day or $5 a year (approximately $3.50 and $70 in 1995 dollars) to enjoy Ravenna's splendid trees and entertaining events. Even with these relatively high fees, 8,000 to 10,000 people visited the park on a busy day.

Sadly, Ravenna's era of private ownership and careful nurturing came to an abrupt end in 1911. As Seattle's population grew, so did sentiment for city parks. Local politicians acquired more land to provide "free access" public parks. Toward this end, the city of Seattle sought to acquire Ravenna Park. The Becks resisted selling because the park was profitable and because they were concerned for the park's amenities. Nonetheless, condemnation proceedings brought Ravenna Park into the public sector for a purchase price of $135,663.

Not long after the transfer to the public domain, the newly created city park changed dramatically. According to newspaper accounts, the giant fir trees in Ravenna began disappearing. The Seattle Federation of Women's Clubs confronted Park Superintendent J. W. Thompson with reports of tree cutting. He conceded that the large "Roosevelt Tree" had been cut down because it had posed a "threat to public safety" and sold for cordwood to defray costs of removal. The federation asked a University of Washington forestry professor to investigate. When the women brought the professor's finding that a number of trees had been cut to the attention of the Park Board, the board expressed regret and promised the cutting would stop. By 1925, however, all the giant fir trees in Ravenna Park had disappeared, replaced by grass, playground equipment, and tennis courts.

Controversy arose over what caused the trees to vanish. Some tried to blame their disappearance on natural causes, such as wind and disease, while others said it was caused by pollution from automobiles and chimney smoke. In fact, it was the bureaucracy that destroyed what the Becks had preserved. Park employees took advantage of their access to the park and cut down the trees to sell as firewood. Park department records charged Superintendent Thompson with abuse of public funds, equipment, and personnel, plus the unauthorized sale of park property.

The lesson from this story is tied to the incentives faced by the two different owners of Ravenna Park. Because the natural beauty was a source of income for the Becks, they preserved it. By destroying the giant trees for immediate gain, they would have received less income, and their wealth would have declined. In contrast, when Ravenna became a city park, these long-term profit incentives vanished. City employees captured short-term gains by cutting and selling the trees. Even an outcry by a watchdog group was unable to prevent their destruction.

Sea Lion Caves

To the south of Seattle, another enviro-capitalist was busy countering government policies that also were destroying natural amenities. On a calm day in 1880, Captain William Cox rowed his small boat into a grotto along the Oregon coast. He was so fascinated with the resident Steller's and California sea lions, bird rookery, and natural greens, pinks, and purples of the cavern walls that he returned to explore it several times. Acting on his instinct that the area was worth preserving, Captain Cox purchased the grotto, known as Sea Lion Caves, in 1887 from the state of Oregon. The property remained in the family until 1926.

The main domed-shaped cavern is about 125 feet high with a floor area of about two acres and is covered with various shades of green, purple, pink, and red from lichens, algae, and minerals. In size and beauty, the caves are reputed to compare to Italy's famous Blue Grotto of Capri. From the top of the headland above the caves, a spectacular ocean vista is favored as a point for viewing killer and gray whales.

In addition to their beauty, the caves and surrounding rocks are the only known breeding and wintering areas of the Steller's sea lion. Approximately two hundred Steller's sea lions reside at the grotto, where they are joined in the fall and winter by another twenty to fifty California sea lions. The area also serves as a rookery for sea birds, most notably Brandt's cormorants and pigeon gillemots.

While owned by the Cox family, the caves remained inaccessible except to the most adventuresome. No consideration was given to wider access until 1927 when R. E. Clanton purchased the grotto with the intent of opening it as a business. Clanton thought the caves would captivate visitors just as it had Captain Cox years earlier. In 1930, Clanton and his two new partners, J. G. Houghton and J. E. Jacobson, risked all that they owned to build a safe access to the grotto. A trail 1,500 feet long was carved by hand into the face of the cliff, and at its lower end, a 135 stair-step wooden tower was extended down to the north entrance of the caves. Sea Lion Caves was opened to the public by this route in August 1932. Visitation increased markedly in 1961 when a 215-foot elevator, designed by the Otis Elevator Company, was constructed. The impact of tourists, however, is minimized by fencing them out while allowing the resident mammals to migrate in and out freely.

Not only have the owners of these caves provided habitat for the Steller's sea lions, they have helped to protect them from hunting. For many years, it was thought that sea lions posed a serious threat to the commercial salmon fishery and therefore had to be exterminated. Toward this end, the state of Oregon paid a bounty of $5 per sea lion killed. The extermination efforts might have been successful if the caves had not provided a safe haven for the sea lions and if the owners had not put a great deal of effort into driving off bounty hunters. Their efforts were eventually combined with legislation to protect sea lions along the Oregon coast.

Today, Sea Lion Caves remains a successful profit-making enterprise, receiving over 200,000 visitors per year. The daily entrance fees are $6 for adults and $4 for children aged six through fifteen. A permanent staff of fifteen employees runs the facility and, during the peak summer season, an additional twenty-five seasonal employees are hired. The Lane Humane Society of Eugene, Oregon, has praised the continuing stewardship of the area. In 1977, Oregon's Governor Robert W. Straub wrote that the property was "one of Oregon's great tourist attractions as well as a great and natural resource." He also lauded its operation because "A private organization has shown that it can, by using a combination of common sense and good management, develop and protect such a great resource and attraction—and still show a profit."

Seeing the Light

In a seminal paper entitled "The Lighthouse in Economics," Nobel Laureate Ronald Coase (1974, 357) described the traditional view that lighthouses had always been provided by the state due to the "impossibility of securing payment from the owners of the ships that benefit from the existence of the lighthouse," thus making "it unprofitable for any private individual or firm to build and maintain a lighthouse." He went on to challenge the market failure view and studied the history of British lighthouses for himself, finding that during lengthy periods in the seventeenth century, no public lighthouses were built at all but "at least ten were built [for profit] by individuals" (Coase 1974, 364). Their owners charged a levy at the local ports, and the government's role was limited "to the establishment and enforcement of property rights in the lighthouse" (Coase 1974, 375).

Just as Coase challenged the conventional wisdom, the history of resource preservation at the turn of the century refutes the standard view of indiscriminate destruction for gain and reveals that envirocapitalists were at work preserving natural and historical amenities for a profit. When entrepreneurs see opportunities to make a profit, they develop innovative contractual arrangements to capitalize on their vision. Certainly not every natural area was preserved, but private, for-profit companies were saving natural areas before the modern conservation movement was in full swing. The potential for private provision is even greater when we consider that other individuals were motivated by their commitment to conservation rather than profits.

Notes

1. See Johnson and Libecap (1980) and Simon (1981).
2. This review of Yellowstone's early entrepreneurs is adapted from a paper by Anderson and Hill (1996).

3. For a colorful discussion of Yankee Jim's toll road, see Whithorn (1989).

4. The fact that loggers were cutting large amount of trees in the Midwest does not necessarily mean that they were violating conservation principles. Economists Johnson and Libecap (1980) show that the rates of timber harvest during this period were efficient given the huge inventory of lumber that existed in the Midwest.

5. Based on the informational brochure "A Brief History of Grandfather Mountain," available from Grandfather Mountain, Linville, North Carolina.

6. The following discussion is adapted from Anderson and Leal (1991, 51–52).

References

Anderson, Terry L. 1990. The Market Process and Environmental Amenities. In *Economics and the Environment: A Reconciliation*, ed. Walter E. Block. Vancouver, British Columbia: Fraser Institute.

Anderson, Terry L., and Peter J. Hill. 1996. Appropriable Rents from Yellowstone Park: A Case of Incomplete Contracting. *Economic Inquiry* 34 (July): 506–18.

Anderson, Terry L., and Donald R. Leal. 1991. *Free Market Environmentalism*. San Francisco: Pacific Research Institute for Public Policy Research.

Bartlett, Richard A. 1974. *Nature's Yellowstone*. Tucson: University of Arizona Press.

Bernstein, Joel H. 1982. *Families That Take in Friends: An Informal History of Dude Ranching*. Stevensville, MT: Stoneydale Press.

Brubaker, Sterling. 1983. Land Use Concepts. In *Governmental Interventions, Social Needs, and the Management of U.S. Forests*, ed. Roger A. Sedjo. Washington, DC: Resources for the Future, 95–114.

Buccholtz, C. W. 1983. *Rocky Mountain National Park: A History*. Boulder: Colorado Associated University Press.

Coase, Ronald H. 1974. The Lighthouse in Economics. *Journal of Law and Economics* 17(2): 1–44.

Earl of Dunraven. 1914. *Canadian Nights*. New York: Charles Scribner's Sons.

———. 1922. *Past Times and Pasttimes*. London: Hodder and Stoughton.

Haines, Aubry L. 1977. *The Yellowstone Story: A History of Our First National Park*. Vols. 1 and 2. Yellowstone National Park, WY: Yellowstone Library and Museum Association.

Ise, John. 1961. *Our National Park Policy: A Critical History*. Baltimore: Johns Hopkins University Press.

Jackson, W. Turrentine. 1957. The Creation of Yellowstone National Park. *Montana: The Magazine of Western History* 7(3): 52–65.

Johnson, Ronald N., and Gary D. Libecap. 1980. *Explorations in Economic History* 17: 276–77.

Kaye, Glen. 1983. Simpler Way of Life Now Gone. *Estes Park Trail*, December 8.

Leopold, Aldo. 1938. *Report on Huron Mountain Club*. Huron, MI: Huron Mountain Club.

Mayor, Archer. 1988. *Huron Mountain Club: The First Hundred Years*. Huron, MI: Huron Mountain Club.

Peterson, Gwen. 1985. *Yellowstone Pioneers: The Story of the Hamilton Stores and Yellowstone National Park*. Yellowstone National Park, WY: Hamilton Stores, Inc.

Runte, Alfred. 1979. *National Parks: The American Experience*. Lincoln: University of Nebraska Press.

———. 1990. *Trains of Discovery*. Niwot, CO: Roberts Rinehart.

Schwantes, Carlos. 1993. *Railroad Signatures across the Pacific Northwest*. Seattle: University of Washington Press.

Simon, Julian. 1981. *The Ultimate Resource*. Princeton, NJ: Princeton University Press.

Whithorn, Doris. 1989. Yankee Jim's National Park Toll Road and the Yellowstone Trail. No publisher, April.

Chapter 3

Mavericks of Conservation

... the initiative of government agencies in large matters of conservation is rare and generally overstated; inertia is the rule.

—Frank Graham Jr., *The Audubon Ark*

While some late nineteenth-century capitalists were profiting from the
preservation of environmental amenities, the seeds of the modern conservation movement were being sown. Leaders such as John Audubon
and John Muir, especially, believed that natural resources were not
being husbanded and that markets were contributing to the problem.
The slaughter of millions of bison, the decimation of bird populations,
and the harvest of ancient trees led them to conclude that market forces
could not be trusted to conserve nature's bounty and, worse, that those
forces would lead to its destruction.

Partly in response to the emerging conservation movement, the national government established a vast political estate that would eventually encompass more than one-third of the nation's lands. The
ostensible purpose of this set-aside was to place these lands under the
authority of scientific managers who would balance uses according to
science rather than profits. This combination of a conservation ethic
and scientific management gave birth to modern environmentalism, as
premised on the idea that good stewardship requires governmental
control of resources.

However, some mavericks in the conservation movement were willing to play within the rules of capitalism. Recognizing that incentives
matter at least as much as ethics, they tried to harness incentives
through private ownership. They bought the conservation movement's
ends, but believed that markets provided a better means to that end.
The enviro-capitalists discussed in this chapter were the mavericks of
conservation.

Rosalie Edge and the Hawk Mountain Sanctuary

Hawk Mountain, located in the Appalachian Mountains of eastern Pennsylvania, derives its name from the tens of thousands of hawks that migrate past the mountain each autumn. The topography and the prevailing winds in the area make Hawk Mountain an ideal place to observe hawks on their southern migration.

Unfortunately, Hawk Mountain once served as a killing field for hawks. Hoards of gunners gathered in the fall on the mountain's top to kill hundreds and even thousands of hawks in a single day. Their actions were legal in Pennsylvania, where most raptors, including hawks, were considered vermin because they preyed on "good" birds. Indeed many state governments and game associations encouraged killing hawks by placing a bounty on them.

A few local conservationists voiced concern about the slaughter at Hawk Mountain as early as 1900, but it was not until the late 1920s that sentiment really began to build for the hawks passing by Hawk Mountain. George M. Sutton, then Pennsylvania's state ornithologist, drew attention to the issue by publishing two articles in a professional journal. Then, in the early 1930s, Richard Plough, an amateur ornithologist, visited Hawk Mountain and began to spread the word about the site to a wider audience of birdwatchers. Plough's efforts were reinforced by Rosalie Edge, a leading conservationist, birdwatcher, and suffragette who had taken up the cause of protecting nongame species.

> She assailed the bird protection organizations of that time for not doing enough. In 1929, she formed the Emergency Conservation Committee and began an active campaign criticizing the "conservation establishment," including the National Association of Audubon Societies, the U.S. Biological Survey, and the state game departments, as being too closely associated with the hunting establishment, sportsmen, and ammunition manufacturers. She argued that these organizations were mainly concerned with the plight of game species: waterfowl, gamebirds, and shorebirds. She maintained that with few exceptions . . . they were relatively indifferent to the fate of many other species. (Smith 1984, 389)

Finding the conservation establishment doing nothing to stop the senseless slaughter at Hawk Mountain, Mrs. Edge took up the cause herself in 1934. One Sunday, she asked Richard Plough to meet her at Hawk Mountain. There they met a real estate agent who was selling 1,398 acres on the mountaintop. She leased the area for one year for

$500 and obtained an option to buy the property for $3,500 (Smith 1984, 389).

Lease in hand, she enlisted the services of a young naturalist named Maurice Broun, who moved to Hawk Mountain and became the site's first warden. Broun arrived on 10 September 1934 and immediately began posting the property and patrolling it to keep hunters out. As far as Broun was concerned, the job was temporary, so he refused to accept a salary that first year. The "temporary" job, however, lasted until 1966.

Despite her initial success, Mrs. Edge found that the leading conservation societies remained indifferent to the cause. Undaunted, she became even more determined to establish Hawk Mountain as a private sanctuary. In 1935, she raised the $3,500 to purchase the 1,398 acres. Three years later, she and her conservation associates established the Hawk Mountain Sanctuary Association, a private, nonprofit, member-supported, conservation organization. The association's mission was to own and manage the Hawk Mountain land.

Rosalie Edge and her maverick associates not only had taken the initial steps to protect birds of prey from senseless slaughter, they also secured a place from which birdwatchers can view these magnificent creatures in flight. The popularity of the sanctuary is indicated by the growing numbers of visitors. In 1935, the first year of operation, the maximum number of visitors on the mountain in a single day was 193. The following year, however, daily visits rose to 540, and today, visitors sometimes exceed 3,000 and come from nearly every state and twenty-five foreign countries to see the fall migration spectacle.

The Hawk Mountain Sanctuary Association itself has grown from a small, unpopular effort to save hawks and other birds of prey into an internationally known conservation, education, and research organization. It has seven full-time and two part-time employees, plus seven to ten interns each year and up to one hundred seasonal volunteers. The association carries out a raptor recovery program in conjunction with state and federal wildlife officials and provides college students, naturalists, and the general public with a better understanding of the role raptors play in ecosystems. The educational effort covers the whole gamut, from displays and field studies available at Hawk Mountain Sanctuary, to courses at local colleges. The association's annual budget of approximately $300,000 comes from membership dues of the 8,500 members and from private contributions of corporate sponsors and individuals. The Hawk Mountain Sanctuary Association maintains a reserve fund of more than $500,000, mostly from large bequests, the revenues from which fund regular operations as well as purchases of additional land to protect the core of the sanctuary.

Hawk Mountain Sanctuary now covers 2,200 acres and receives approximately 70,000 visitors per year. Entrance is free to members, but nonmembers pay $4.00 for adults and $2.00 for children between six and twelve years of age. In addition to providing a spectacular area to view raptors, the sanctuary preserves a large block of continuous deciduous forest in the Appalachian Mountains that is home to white-tailed deer, ruffed grouse, wild turkey, and red and gray fox. A marked trail leads visitors to a number of bird-watching points, including the popular North Lookout, at an elevation of 1,500 feet above sea level. The history of Hawk Mountain is a classic example of what can be accomplished by a few dedicated individuals using the security of private property to protect species.

A Hot Family Tradition

From one early successful bird rescue we move to another on Avery Island. The island is one of five rising above the bayou country of Louisiana. It has been privately owned for 175 years, mostly by the descendants of the McIlhenny family. Its rich soil sits atop a mountain of salt as deep as Mount Everest is high. In addition to exporting oil and salt, the island is best known as the birthplace of world-famous Tabasco pepper sauce. Less well known are the private wildlife refuge teeming with thousands of birds, deer, bears, alligators, muskrats, nutrias, and foxes; an ancient forest of 1,300-year-old oak trees; and a beautiful jungle garden, replete with native and exotic plant species.

Avery Island was also the site of a crucial effort to protect the snowy egret from extinction (McIlhenny Company 1968, 18). In the late nineteenth century, the egret was threatened by hunters who sought the birds' valuable plumage. The egret rescue effort was spearheaded by Edward Avery McIlhenny, Edmund McIlhenny's eldest son and a dedicated naturalist. After several years away from the island on an Arctic expedition, E. A. returned to the island in 1892. What he found distressed him greatly. The snowy egrets, those exquisite birds that had always nested by the thousands in the Louisiana swamps surrounding Avery Island, were all but gone, killed by hunters for their special feathers, the aigrettes used to adorn ladies' hats and hairdos.

McIlhenny was determined to rescue the snowy egret. After searching for weeks in the early summer, he finally found eight egret chicks and took them to Avery Island. He succeeded in raising these birds and released them that fall to migrate south across the Gulf of Mexico. The following spring, six egrets returned to form the nucleus egret colony that ornithologists credit with saving the bird from extinction. The colony grew rapidly and today numbers in the tens of thousands.

It was an outstanding achievement by a dedicated conservationist, but it wasn't his only conservation achievement on the island. While presiding for forty years over the growing Tabasco business, E. A. continued his conservation efforts. He wrote numerous articles and books on natural history, including a book about Bird City, the name given his snowy egret sanctuary on Avery Island. He banded 189,289 snowy egrets so he could track their migratory routes and developed his land into a sanctuary for many other wildlife species. E. A. McIlhenny also planted a beautiful 200-acre garden that today provides one of the island's most scenic amenities.

This is an area lush with azaleas, irises, and camellias that bloom in early spring of each year. In this garden, McIlhenny planted Chinese and Japanese wisteria, hedges of Oriental holly and 64 varieties of bamboo. Lotus and pappus from the Nile were imported for small pools, and McIlhenny achieved a design of color and symmetry that has made the gardens as famous as the scarlet peppers of the Tabasco sauce industry. (Moore 1990, 9)

Though oil was discovered on the edge of the island in 1942, the 100 wells drilled since then have been developed in accordance with strict conservation practices. The developer, Humble Oil, cooperated fully with the demands made by the family that they carry out their work in a manner that preserved the wildlife and natural beauty of the island. For example, all pipelines are buried so that the usual equipment surrounding an oilfield is hardly visible. Mud pits are filled and sodded over, and rail fences are placed around well frames to prevent wildlife from harming themselves (Moore 1990, 14). According to Edward (Ned) McIlhenny Simmons, grandson of E. A. and current president of McIlhenny Company, these practices were carried out decades before Congress enacted environmental regulations on oil development. Oil production is declining now, and the McIlhenny family plans to turn the oil production field into another wildlife sanctuary—a fitting conclusion to years of sensitive development.

The McIlhenny family takes great pride in its long-term protection of Avery Island's amenities. Testimony to their stewardship is seen today through the eyes of over 100,000 annual visitors to the island. For a modest fee of $5.25 for adults and $3.75 for children from ages six to twelve, visitors can enjoy E. A. McIlhenny's beautiful Jungle Gardens as well as watch thousands of snowy egrets at Bird City. The gate receipts profit the wildlife and enable the family to accommodate the tourists.

Maverick Aldo Leopold

Aldo Leopold is mostly famous for his "land ethic," described in his best-known writing on the subject, *A Sand County Almanac*. This book is a poetic masterpiece of ecology and ethics that has won him adulation throughout the conservation community.[1] Indeed, he may be the most widely quoted philosopher-naturalist of our times. In his classic essay, "The Land Ethic," he wrote, "A land ethic, then, reflects the existence of an ecological conscience, and this in turn reflects a conviction of individual responsibility for the health of the land" (Leopold 1971, 258).

Not so widely appreciated is Leopold's appreciation for the power of market forces. Throughout his career, Leopold wrestled with how economics "both motivates and constrains land use decisions" (Palmini 1993, 38). He was by no means sanguine that markets could address all conservation problems, but neither did he blindly accept government action as the only response (Leopold 1971, 249). Importantly, Leopold recognized the important role of the individual landowner.

Leopold began practicing what he preached when he acquired an abandoned farm in Sauk County, Wisconsin, that ultimately served as inspiration for the ideas articulated in *A Sand County Almanac*. In 1937, Leopold purchased the farm to serve as a retreat from his duties as the country's first professor of wildlife management at the University of Wisconsin and to test whether land depleted from years of intensive use could be restored to health. The farm had been heavily logged and farmed from the mid-nineteenth century into the early twentieth century. Like thousands of other farms in the Midwest, it was in very poor condition. Leopold spent weekends there with his family, staying in a small run-down cabin known as the "shack." During their stays, the family planted thousands of trees, and Leopold himself tested a number of ideas on how the land could be restored by initiating nature's own recuperative powers. The results showed that with "intelligent tinkering," you could indeed return the land to biological productivity.

As a maverick of conservation, Aldo Leopold questioned the growing trend in the United States to rely mainly on government for conservation. He came to view such a reliance as a "band-aid" approach (quoted in Palmini 1993, 41). In addressing the limits of government he wrote, "We tried to get conservation by buying land, by subsidizing desirable land changes in land use, and by passing restrictive laws. The last method largely failed; the other two have produced some small samples of success" (Leopold 1991, 193–94).

Leopold was also one of the first to steer attention toward the all-important role of private conservation. "I do challenge the growing assumption that bigger buying [of public land] is a substitute for private conservation practice" (Leopold 1991, 196). He wanted to change how private land was used in commodity production so that more habitat would be available for wildlife. To Leopold, a key to changing behavior was giving the private landowner an economic stake in conservation. In his essay "Conservation Economics," he concludes that "conservation will ultimately boil down to rewarding the private land-owner who conserves the public interest" (Leopold 1991, 202).

Today the Leopold legacy lives on through the entirely private 1,500-acre Leopold Memorial Reserve, owned and managed by the Sand County Foundation. The reserve includes the farm from which Leopold derived his ideas. The Sand County Foundation, a private, non-profit organization established in September 1965, created the reserve and oversees its restoration. The reserve itself serves as an experimental laboratory for testing new methods of restoring natural ecological processes on lands that have been intensively farmed or logged, damaged, and abandoned. Included are cultivated lands, oak savannas, sedge meadows, prairie grasslands, and wetlands that provide habitat for wildlife.

Apart from the original farm, tracts of land have been incorporated into the reserve's management system through agreements with neighboring landowners. Each of the owners participating in the reserve has agreed to refrain from certain land use practices detrimental to the restoration of natural habitats. Landowners retain title to their property and agree to manage individual parcels in concert with the objectives of the entire reserve. The original agreement bound landowners to a five-year term, to be extended indefinitely unless formally terminated by a majority of the landowners who were party to the agreement. By the agreement, participating landowners take a pro-active

approach toward restoring the natural amenities. They maintain a prescribed fire management program to enhance soil vitality and forest
understory growth; carry out selective timber cuts to increase biological diversity; conduct planting programs to supplement natural habitat
and wildlife foods; sponsor baseline inventory and peer-reviewed research; and carry out a coordinated trespass control program to protect
the area from vandalism, poaching, and littering. In addition, the landowners allow the Sand County Foundation's scientific team of ecolo-
gists, biologists, and hydrologists to monitor and manage the reserve
as a single unit.

In establishing these arrangements, the foundation took to heart Leopold's words on compensating landowners. Reed Coleman, Sand
County's chairman, describes how this was done.

> A couple of us decided we ought to do something about curtailing devel-
> opment near the shack. We went to seven or eight landowners of various
> types and convinced them to enter into a voluntary agreement. . . . As
> compensation, we would pay that landowner's property taxes. We devel-
> oped these agreements in 1965, before conservation easements had been
> discovered, and they have lasted almost thirty years. (Coleman 1994, 19)

The Sand County Foundation uses the reserve as an important vehi-
cle to convey its message of land stewardship. According to its 1989
brochure, the foundation is

> in the practice of healing the biologic community, with its human popula-
> tion on the lands and waters of the northeastern Sauk County, Wisconsin.
> We do so to provide one model of effective stewardship. This is not to
> generate precise replicas, but in order to enable other private landowners
> and committed conservationists to find their own way back to the good
> earth.

Education on the reserve includes primary-school visits, invited conservation "working tours," and seminars for corporate leaders. At
every level, the foundation emphasizes participating in active conservation work on private lands. Adult visitors to the reserve enjoy Leopold's practical approach to conservation that lets them get their hands
dirty. Recent projects include picking and sacking of prairie seeds for
prairie restoration, surveying of tracts for weedy plants and removing
them, and assisting with the prescribed fires.

When compared to the paucity of wildlife in the 1930s, the success of
the ongoing restoration program is impressive. The reserve now boasts

resident bald eagles, otters, black bears, and deer. Meanwhile, continual monitoring of the reserve and the various conservation practices provide a long-term experiment in land management. By virtue of private, voluntary action, the landowners are finding ways to use good stewardship to enhance the biological diversity of their land. For other landowners interested in protecting natural amenities and enhancing the long-term productivity of their land, the reserve provides an effective tool for practical environmental education.

In the maverick spirit of Leopold, the foundation continues to test new ideas in restoration under the direction of Brent Haglund, its president. One of Haglund's recent creations is the "Quality Hunting Ecology Program," which links wildlife management to ecosystem improvement. Recognizing that too many deer will disrupt ecological balances and that most hunters want to shoot buck deer, the program controls deer population on the reserve and adjacent private land by requiring hunters earn a buck by first harvesting two does.[2] The success of the program is demonstrated by (1) the increase in the number of indicator species such as white pine and white oak, whose recruitment is essentially nil throughout the Midwest because deer overbrowse the saplings; (2) the improved age and sex ratio of the deer population; and (3) better resource stewardship by landowners who take more interest in wildlife habitat and hunters who litter and vandalize less and spend more time enjoying their hunting. Under Haglund's leadership, the program is being implemented on thousands of acres of Wisconsin Power & Light Company and Champion International Corporation lands, resulting in reduced land management costs and improved hunting opportunities.

Similarly, innovative experiments with prescribed burns and designed tree harvests on the Leopold Memorial Reserve are now being used on other lands in Wisconsin. A key project entails restoration of oak savannas. This type of habitat has dwindled in the Midwest because years of fire suppression have hampered natural regeneration. Haglund and researchers at the Sand County Foundation are reversing this trend by coordinating the efforts of different landowners in Wisconsin to regain thousands of acres of oak savannas through the use of prescribed fire management and timber cutting.[3] The foundation's researchers provide scientific advice to landowners such as the Wisconsin Electric Power Company, the Department of the Army at Fort McCoy, and the U.S. Fish and Wildlife Service at Necedah National Wildlife Refuge, Wisconsin Power & Light Company, the Nature Conservancy, Wisconsin Department of Natural Resources, and U.S. Forest

Service at the Chequamegan National Forest. This includes suggestions on how fire can be used in combination with selective logging to increase habitat for the endangered Karner blue butterfly.

Leopold found private property suitable for putting his nontraditional ideas to work, and that approach continues today with the Leopold Memorial Reserve and the Sand County Foundation. As Brent Haglund put it when asked about the efficacy of governmental programs to preserve wildlife habitat, "You know what I like? A deed in the courthouse." Private property rights offer entrepreneurs like Aldo Leopold and Rosalie Edge the security to swim against the tide of popular and scientific opinion to preserve natural resources.

A Penchant for Peregrines

Just as early enviro-capitalists rejected the conventional wisdom about conservation, so have a few contemporary birders, including Dr. Tom Cade. His efforts to save peregrine falcons represent one of the most successful bird recovery stories in recent years.

The peregrine falcon is one of the most spectacular hawk species in North America and Europe. Standing about eighteen inches high with a wingspan of four feet, it is has been clocked at speeds of nearly 200 miles an hour. Because it is a fierce predator, it is the species most favored by falconers. Unfortunately, like many other birds of prey in the United States, peregrines experienced a long, slow decline due to government extermination programs, habitat loss, and egg collecting. After World War II, the falcon's decline accelerated. By 1960, not a single breeding pair of peregrines lived east of the Mississippi, and western populations had dwindled to a small fraction of their prewar population levels. The likely causes of the decline after World War II were the pesticides DDT and dieldrin, both of which were popular through the 1950s and 1960s. DDT caused reproductive failure of peregrines, and dieldrin was implicated in the toxic deaths of adult peregrines.

By the time the government banned the use of these pesticides in the early 1970s and extended protection to peregrines under authority of the Migratory Bird Treaty Act and the Endangered Species Act, it was almost too late. These laws protected the survivors, but in areas where the peregrine was endangered, the laws were not enough. An innovative breeding and release effort was needed to help the bird recover in the wild.

In the late 1960s, when falconers recognized that wild populations were in peril, they began breeding peregrines in captivity without government support to ensure a continuous supply for their sport. This required capturing a few birds in the wild for breeding stock, an idea that was not very popular among environmentalists and bureaucrats. By the early 1970s, the breeding programs were successful enough to have a sustainable breeding stock. At the same time, Tom Cade, a professor of ornithology at Cornell University, founded the private, nonprofit organization known as the Peregrine Fund and instituted a program of captive propagation and restoration, building on and improving the breeding techniques developed by falconers. "Essentially, Cade's concept was to institute a regular breeding operation that would eventually produce enough peregrines to restore the species throughout its former range. . . . His breeding stock initially consisted of birds donated or lent by falconers and wild birds from the Arctic, the Pacific Northwest, Europe, South America, and Australia (Smith 1990, 357).

The accomplishments of the peregrine breeding and restorations program are astounding. Between 1974 and 1992, 4,045 peregrines were released throughout North America (Urbanski 1992, 106). In 1991, releases in the East ended because peregrine populations had successfully reached their carrying capacity in many areas and were dispersing to new areas and breeding on their own. Considerable progress was also made in the West. As a result, the Peregrine Fund considers the peregrine falcon to be virtually "recovered" in the United States.

Today, Cade and the Peregrine Fund's headquarters are located in Boise, Idaho, because of the raptor habitat in the area. Southern Idaho supports the world's densest breeding populations of eagles, hawks, falcons, and owls. The new facility was named the World Center for Birds of Prey to reflect the Peregrine Fund's broader commitment to restoring birds of prey throughout the world. The fund is now in the process of developing innovative recovery techniques to restore the endangered Aplomado falcon in the southwestern United States, the endangered Alala or Hawaiian crow in Hawaii, the very rare Mauritius kestrel on the island of Mauritius, and the Harpy eagle in Mexico and Central America. Peregrines are still being bred in Boise and released in the Rocky Mountain and Pacific Northwest. The propagation and reintroduction techniques developed and perfected by the Peregrine Fund have been so successful that both conservation and government agencies are applying them in programs aimed at restoring other threatened birds.

Just over two-thirds of the Peregrine Fund's fiscal 1995 operating budget of $3.3 million comes from individuals, companies, and private foundations.[4] The remaining funding comes from government agencies for the support of selected captive breeding projects that will supply the government with certain species, such as the California condor, for release in the wild. The Peregrine Fund is proud that its administrative costs constitute only a very small part of its total spending. Nearly ninety cents of every dollar in contributions is spent on bird recovery projects, thus substantiating the organization's claim that "We work hard, we stretch donations, and we get results—no fluffs, no frills, just solid conservation" (Peregrine Fund 1992).

The Peregrine Fund's growing record of success is testimony to what can be accomplished through private initiative, but at times its efforts have been hindered by government regulation and bureaucratic bungling. From the early days of the peregrine breeding program, the delivery of falcons to and from the original location in Ithaca, New York, was stymied by burdensome paperwork and a slow process for getting transportation permits under the Endangered Species Act. Meanwhile, the government's attempts at breeding peregrine falcons at the Patuxent Wildlife Research Center in Maryland were proving unsuccessful. Eventually, thanks to the delivery of birds from falconers and from foreign sources, the Peregrine Fund was able to obtain the birds it needed to start its recovery program.

Similar burdensome regulations hinder the fund's international recovery efforts. Many of the projects at the Idaho center require permits to import birds from foreign nations under authority of the Convention on International Trade in Endangered Species (CITES). In the United States, the permitting process as administered by the Fish and Wildlife Service often takes months, which in turn hinders the timing of deliveries to match reproduction periods and adds to transportation stresses. To avoid such problems, projects such as the recovery of the Mauritius kestrels have been moved out of the United States and are being conducted at foreign sites that are more expensive (Peregrine Fund 1992). Fortunately, entrepreneurs such as Tom Cade have the energy to keep working despite these hurdles.

The Bird Man of Big Timber

Another high-octane bird rescuer is Montanan Bob Elgas. His sixty-acre wildlife refuge echoes with the raucous noise of its avian residents, the loudest of which are the hyacinth macaws. These rare and beautiful creatures from Central and South America emit loud screeching sounds whenever a stranger enters their domain.

Elgas says that the hyacinths' shrill cries may one day be silent in their old haunts in the Amazon Basin in South America and in the rain forests of Central America. Habitat loss from development and an onslaught from bird-nappers who sell them to pet stores have contributed to their precipitous decline. For example, in the last fifteen years the population of macaws has dropped from a quarter million to 5,000 under the green canopy of the Amazon Basin in Brazil.

Bob Elgas is trying to ensure that hyacinth macaws and other rare birds will be around in the future. He has no formal education in the study of birds but is not deterred. "I just read and studied," he says. His lack of formal training has not hampered the success he has had rearing macaws and other rare birds on his refuge. In addition to hyacinths, Elgas has rare buffon's macaws, emperor geese, greylag geese (the wild European ancestor of domestic geese), and western bean geese, of which there are only ten in the United States.

He also has Tule geese, whose genus carries his name. When he first started studying geese, none of the professionals believed that they were a separate species. Elgas finally got permission to study them in California and, after five years, captured a live one and supervised the detailed analysis that showed it was a separate species. The Smithsonian described the goose and named it "Anser albifrons elgasi" after the Big Timber, Montana, aviculturist. Elgas followed his California fieldwork with an expedition to Cook Inlet in Alaska, where he found the geese breeding ground and obtained goslings for future breeding. Today descendants of those original birds roam the refuge grounds.

Elgas has recently cut back on the flock of captive birds he keeps on the refuge so he can devote more time to breeding macaws, whose future he believes is dim. The birds hatch their own eggs and take care of the chicks for the first two weeks. Then Elgas takes them away to rear under conditions designed to increase survival. For example, he uses old incubators obtained from a local hospital in Billings to keep the chicks warm until they reach an age when they can generate their own body heat. Until then, he feeds the chicks with a concoction of ground sunflower seeds, peanuts, prepared seed, Gerber's baby cereal, fruit, vegetables, and special nutrient-rich feed blended to the consistency of pancake batter and warmed to exactly 105 degrees Fahrenheit. He feeds them by filling a syringe with the concoction and shooting it down their throats.

Elgas is not the only one dedicated to improving the lot of rare birds. He is, in fact, part of a worldwide network of private breeders whose goal is to establish captive, self-sustaining populations of rare birds. According to the International Wild Waterfowl Association, an organization established in 1958, some 500 members take an active role in private captive breeding programs for rare waterfowl and other rare species of birds. In addition to donating time and money to their own captive breeding projects, many of these individuals work together to produce books and wildlife art for educating the public about wild bird species. *The Colored Key to Waterfowl of the World, The Waterfowl of North America, Grouse and Quail of North America,* and *Raising Wild Geese in Captivity* are but a few of the books that have been published and sold to the public. The dollars raised from the sale of these and other books and wildlife art prints help support ongoing efforts of captive breeders (Greenwell and Kiracofe 1993, 12).

For Elgas, conserving birds is a labor of love. He pays for care of his macaws and other birds through the sale of common parrot species raised on his refuge and through the sale of his wildlife paintings. He has spent the better part of his adult life rearing rare birds with much success. Both he and his wife, Elizabeth, were recently inducted into the International Wild Waterfowl Association's Waterfowl Breeders Hall of Fame. Still, he is quite humble about his accomplishments. "You can cover a lot of sins by being determined," he says. "Sometimes you find success because you are too stubborn to admit defeat" (Thackeray 1993). Spoken like a true entrepreneur.

Out of Africa and into Texas

Jim Jackson and Christine Jurzykowski and their staff of naturalists and veterinarians run the Fossil Rim Wildlife Center, located about eighty miles south of Dallas. Its 2,700 acres of rolling hills and grasslands make it an ideal sanctuary for beleaguered wildlife from around the globe. The white rhino, threatened by poaching in Africa, finds safe haven at Fossil Rim. The nearly extinct Attwater's prairie chicken, the rare red wolf, Gravy's zebra, and the scimitar-horned oryx (extinct in the wild) all thrive there.

The Fossil Rim staff hopes that these animals are taking their first steps toward recovering in the wild. Research and breeding programs there focus on saving species before they are lost to future generations and one day repopulating them in the wilds. Staff naturalists and veterinarians are helping threatened species overcome the threat of extinction. Gail Rankin, vice president of communications, says, "Our goal is to see all animals returned to their natural habitat" (quoted in Mueller 1994).

Fossil Rim's record speaks for itself. Since receiving its first pair of red wolves in 1989, the facility has had nineteen surviving births, paving the way for the red wolf's successful reintroduction into the wild. Eighty-seven cheetahs have been born at Fossil Rim. This is impressive, considering that worldwide, more cheetahs die than are born every year in the wild. Many Fossil Rim cheetahs have been given to zoos or other captive breeding programs so that those groups will not take wild cheetahs for their stocking programs. Fossil Rim also has successfully bred addax antelope into a herd of 100, believed to be the largest in the world.

Though most of its efforts focus on animals in trouble, Fossil Rim also devotes resources to conservation efforts in native habitats. For example, the center has contributed staff to study habitat needs of the cotton top tamarin (a multicolored monkey) in Colombia and donated several trucks to the Chihuahua Bioreserve in Mexico.

The story behind Fossil Rim is one of both altruism and entrepreneurship. In the early 1970s, oilman Tom Mantzel purchased 1,400 acres of what was then Waterfall Ranch, an exotic game ranch. He wanted to turn it into a sanctuary for a growing list of rare animals and soon gathered sixteen nonnative or endangered species on the property. Fossil Rim Wildlife Ranch, as Mantzel renamed it, became the first ranch to participate in the Species Survival Plan of the American Association of Zoological Parks and Aquariums. By 1984, however, the American petroleum industry had collapsed, and the Texas economy was suffering.

Mantzel needed money to support his hobby, so he opened the preserve to the public for a fee. He built a 9.5-mile road through the hills and pastures so that people could drive through and observe the wildlife from a distance. He added a snack bar and a souvenir store. Volunteers guided an ever-increasing number of schoolchildren, scouts, and families through the refuge.

Mounting oil losses forced Mantzel to take on two partners. A well-off couple, Jim Jackson and Christine Jurzykowski, did not come from a conservation background, but they were looking for a way to make a difference in conservation. At first, they supplied funds to keep the ranch operating, but in 1987 they bought Fossil Rim outright.

Under their direction, Fossil Rim has made great strides. It grew from 1,400 to 2,700 acres, and its animal population increased from 500 to 1,100 encompassing thirty-two species. Not all are endangered, but all serve to bring in paying tourists to support the refuge.

On the staff are naturalists and veterinarians who carry out a variety of groundbreaking projects. For example, the staff is working to perfect reproductive technologies to create a larger gene pool for the addax antelope. They also carry out captive breeding research of white rhino, using a "teaser" male in one enclosure to encourage breeding by a male in an adjacent one. Fossil Rim researchers are testing techniques for reversible contraception that controls animal populations in captivity but that can be reversed when they are released into the wild.

To finance this work, Jackson and Jurzykowski use their entrepreneurial imagination to capitalize on various revenue sources. The big money-maker is still the drive-through tour, for which 105,000 people per year pay $12.95 ($9.95 for children three to eleven years old). In addition to the 9.5-mile tour, they expanded to offer safari-style overnight vacation packages. There is the Foothills Safari Camp, packaged especially for "safari" goers. Its seven tents accommodate a maximum of fourteen adult guests, except on special family weekends when children are allowed. This camp is not exactly an African safari of old. Each tent has twin beds, central air-conditioning and heat, ceiling fan, private bathroom with shower, southwestern decor, and a patio with chairs. Meals are taken in a pavilion with large windows for viewing wildlife. Menus include blackened rib-eye steak, and chicken with cranberry and peach chutney, as well as delicious desserts. Weather permitting, campers enjoy gourmet meals around the campfire. Rates are $150 per tent per night. The less adverturesome may choose the bed-and-breakfast lodge at Fossil Rim, overlooking hills and meadows filled with wildlife.

Like many young enterprises, making ends meet was difficult at first, but perservance and imagination by these two enviro-capitalists are paying off. In 1992, revenues from tourism topped $2.2 million, but Jackson and Jurzykowski still had to make up the $400,000 difference between revenues and expenses. In 1996, Fossil Rim made its first profit.

Adopt a Pothole

With nesting habitat the key, the problem for North American waterfowl is how to make farming compatible with waterfowl production.

Delta Waterfowl, under the direction of Charles Potter, has implemented some innovative solutions.

Potter recognized a need to act when he noted a precipitous decline
in migratory duck populations. Between the 1950s and the 1980s,
North American duck migrations fell from over 100 million to less than
50 million. This decline has been of grave concern to hunters and biologists. Ironically, the decline has occurred despite years of increasingly
stringent hunting regulations, as well as the establishment of 430 national wild refuges, totaling some 90 million acres, in the continental
United States. Research indicates that duck populations dwindled because of the loss of nesting habitat, mainly on thousands of private
farms in the upper midwestern United States and in southern Canada.
This area, known as the prairie pothole region, covers some 300,000
square miles and is one of the world's richest agricultural regions. Because it is dotted by millions of Ice Age depressions that create small
ponds, the prairie pothole region produces the majority of North
American ducks.

Delta Waterfowl is a private, nonprofit organization dedicated to reversing the trend in North American duck populations by stopping the
loss of habitat. The organization believes it can make a difference
through research and education and by creating economic incentives
for farmers to produce ducks as well as crops. Support for the organization comes entirely from the tax-deductible contributions of individuals, companies, conservation organizations, and private foundations.

Research and education are carried out at the Delta Waterfowl and
Wetlands Research Station, located in south central Manitoba, on the
famed 50,000-acre Delta Marsh. Over the last sixty years, the station
has made many critical contributions to the study of waterfowl and
wetlands in North America. For example, research at the station developed new surveying and banding techniques and improved methods
for increasing waterfowl nesting success. Delta Waterfowl and Wetlands Station researchers have published more than sixty scientific pa-
pers and books and have trained many university and government
scientists.

The station was the brainchild of James Ford Bell, chairman of General Mills during the 1930s and avid duck hunter and conservationist.
In the late 1920s, he purchased a significant portion of Delta Marsh as
a private hunting preserve and wild duck hatchery. Several years later,
he converted the marsh into a waterfowl and wetlands research station
on the advice of Dr. Miles Pirnie, a professor in wildlife management
at Michigan State University, and Aldo Leopold. In 1949, Bell pre-

sented the Delta Marsh property, the hatchery and research facilities, and a generous contribution for operational support to the North American Wildlife Foundation, now known as Delta Waterfowl.

In recent years, Delta Waterfowl, under the direction of Charles Potter, has unveiled grass-roots projects, including the Prairie Farming Program, aimed at enhancing waterfowl production on farms in the midwestern region of the United States and Canada. This program has studied new soil and water conservation practices that are both economically and biologically sound. Because Delta Waterfowl understands its programs will not be adopted by farmers if they are not economical, it always emphasizes profitability.

With profitability in mind, the foundation established its innovative Adopt a Pothole program in 1991. Through this program, Delta Waterfowl contracts with farmers to produce ducks by protecting the nesting habitat around prairie potholes on their land. This approach differs markedly from the federal government's strategy of acquiring land for refuges or regulating private wetland use. Delta Waterfowl believes that the Adopt a Pothole program can make a significant impact because 95 percent of the ducks raised on the prairies of the upper Midwest and southern Canada are produced on private farmlands. Prior to the program, landowners had little or no economic incentive to maintain or restore pothole habitat and may have even faced a disincentive from government farm programs that subsidized draining potholes.[5] As a result, over the last fifty years, hundreds of thousands of acres of potential duck factories have been lost.

Delta Waterfowl believes that farmers must be sent a different message, one based on positive incentives, and it has done this through its Adopt a Pothole program. This program is a classic example of envirocapitalism because it takes advantage of all aspects of entrepreneurship. First, the Delta entrepreneurs discovered a niche that was not being filled by existing public and private waterfowl conservation programs. Second, Adopt a Pothole created a way of raising capital from hundreds of individual contributors in the United States and Canada by giving them a sense of ownership in a pothole. Each contributor receives an aerial photograph of his or her adopted pothole, a quarterly reports on its status, and an annual estimate of duck production. Third, Adopt a Pothole achieves its goal through innovative contractual arrangements consisting of multiyear land leases and production contracts. The land leases pay farmers approximately $7 per acre to maintain pothole habitat and $30 per acre to restore pothole habitat. Production contracts pay directly for duck production, thus giving the farmer an incentive to invest in improving nesting habitat.

The program has been overwhelmingly successful both in terms of raising capital and duck production. Contributions totaled over $2.5 million after four years of operation, and the list of leased sites grew from forty in 1991 to over 1,400 in 1994 (Potter 1994). These sites are located on farms in Manitoba, Minnesota, and North Dakota, providing nesting habitat for mallards, canvasbacks, shovelers, bluewinged teals, greenwinged teals, gadwalls, lesser scaups, redheads, and pintails. They are fast becoming North America's duck factories. For instance, nest density is twice as great for adopted sites compared to unadopted sites, and nesting success averages 51 percent for adopted sites compared to 10–15 percent for unadopted ones. Moreover, for those adopted potholes that use a special Delta Waterfowl nesting device that better protects nests from predators, nesting success was an astounding 90 percent (Delta Waterfowl 1993). Such early accomplishments have earned the program accolades from the conservation community. On 8 June 1994, the U.S. Wildlife Service awarded the Adopt a Pothole program its National Wetlands Conservation Award for the prairie pothole region (Delta Waterfowl 1994).

Going Private

As these case studies demonstrate, nonprofit maverick entrepreneurs have made significant contributions to conservation over the last hundred years, and they can contribute much more. At a time when our national parks, wildlife refuges, and wilderness areas are experiencing growing budget shortfalls accompanied by overcrowding, we must explore alternatives in the private sector. Ornithologist and policy analyst R. J. Smith puts it this way: "In an earlier day, government land managers devoted much of their time to the protection of game species from overhunting; now they increasingly have to protect lands and wildlife from over-camping, over-littering, over-trampling, over-disturbing, and even over-watching (Smith 1984, 366). As early as 1934, Leopold recognized the overcrowding problem:

> The more people are concentrated on a given area, the less is the chance of their finding what they seek. This is not true of the uncritical mob, but I see no more reason for running a national or state park to please the mob than a public art gallery or a public university. A slum is a slum, whether in the Bowery or on the Yellowstone. (Leopold 1991, 196)

As long as the price of using these areas is kept low, underfunding and overcrowding will only get worse.

These problems are reduced when protection of amenities is carried out with strictly private efforts. For example, the 13,000-acre Pine Butte Preserve in northwest Montana, privately owned and managed by the Nature Conservancy, provides critical habitat for grizzly bears when they come out of the high country in the spring to replenish themselves after a long winter's hibernation. Because it is privately operated, the preserve's managers are free to keep human use at a minimum during this critical period (see Dodge 1990, 3 and 33).

On a much broader scale, the geographical and biological importance of private lands in America cannot be overlooked in the provision of biodiversity. Approximately 60 percent of the area of the United States is in private ownership, with the greatest concentrations in the East. Moreover, these private lands include the best habitat. The stream bottoms, the wetlands, the springs, and the grasslands were among the areas first chosen by the private owner. Because scientists agree that these are the most biologically diverse, we must follow Leopold's advice by "rewarding the private landowner who conserves the public interest."

Notes

1. *A Sand County Almanac* was published posthumously in 1949 and sold only 20,000 copies between 1948 and 1968. But since then, the book has grown immensely in popularity, surpassing Rachel Carson's *Silent Spring*, Stuart Udall's *Quiet Crisis*, and Barry Commoner's *Closing Circle* as the "philosophical touchstone of the modern environmental movement" (see Flader and Callicott 1991, ix).

2. Telefax transmittal from the Sand County Foundation, 28 July 1995.

3. Telefax transmittal from the Sand County Foundation, 28 July 1995.

4. Information provided by Jeff Cilek of the Peregrine Fund.

5. See Anderson and Leal (1991, 57) for further discussion of the impact of farm subsidies.

References

Anderson, Terry L., and Donald R. Leal. 1991. *Free Market Environmentalism.* San Francisco: Pacific Institute for Public Policy Research.

Coleman, Reed. 1994. The Land Ethic in Modern Times. *Philanthropy,* fall.

Delta Waterfowl. 1993. *Delta Waterfowl: Adopt a Pothole Summary Report*, August.

———. 1994. Adopt a Pothole Named Top Waterfowl Program on the Prairies. *Delta Waterfowl Report*, fall.

Dodge, Sue E., ed. 1990. *Nature Conservancy*, March–April.

Flader, Susan L., and J. Baird Callicott, eds. 1991. *The River of the Mother of God and Other Essays by Aldo Leopold*. Madison: University of Wisconsin Press.

Graham, Frank, Jr. 1990. *The Audubon Ark: A History of the National Audubon Society*. New York: Knopf.

Greenwell, Guy, and Jack and Viola Kiracofe. 1993. *The International Wild Waterfowl Association, Inc.: History of Achievement, 1958–1992*. Lee, NH: International Wild Waterfowl Association.

Leopold, Aldo. 1971. The Land Ethic. In *A Sand County Almanac with Essays on Conservation from Round River*. Reprint. New York: Ballantine Books.

———. 1991. Conservation Economics [1934]. In *The River of the Mother of God and Other Essays by Aldo Leopold*, ed. Susan L. Flader and J. Baird Callicott. Madison: University of Wisconsin Press, 193–202.

McIlhenny Company. 1968. *The 100 Year History of Tabasco*. Avery Island, LA: McIlhenny Company.

Moore, Diane M. 1990. *The Treasures of Avery Island*. Lafayette, LA: Acadian House Publishing.

Mueller, Gene. 1994. Rare Species Find a Home on the Range. *Insight*, October 17.

Palmini, Dennis J. 1993. The Conservation Economics of Aldo Leopold. *Wisconsin Academy Review* (summer): 37–44.

Peregrine Fund. 1992. *Annual Report, 1992*. Boise, ID: Peregrine Fund/World Center for Birds of Prey.

Potter, Charles S. 1994. Editorial. *Delta Waterfowl Report*, April–May.

Smith, Robert J. 1984. Special Report: The Public Benefits of Private Conservation. In *Environmental Quality, 15th Annual Report of the Council on Environmental Quality*. Washington, DC: Council on Environmental Quality, 363–429.

———. 1990. Private Solutions to Conservation Problems. In *The Theory of Market Failure*, ed. Tyler Cowen. Fairfax, VA: George Mason University Press, 341–60.

Thackeray, Lorna. 1993. One Man's Passion May Be Last Hope for Endangered Birds. *Billings Gazette*, November 4.

Urbanski, Mark. 1992. Birds and Birding: A Case of Private Provision. Working paper 92-19. Bozeman, MT: Political Economy Research Center.

Chapter 4

The Business of Bambi

Compensate him [the landowner] directly or indirectly for producing a game crop. . . .

—Aldo Leopold
American Game Conference, 1930

The "conventional story" of wildlife in the marketplace is not a positive one. For example, recall the plight of the snowy egret on Avery Island in the late 1800s (chapter 3). The wanton slaughter of these birds and other species such as the bison and passenger pigeon is a blight on the history of North America's wildlife management. The slaughter is often blamed on the markets for meat, hides, and feathers that induced hunters to kill for profit.

The market for dead wildlife, which marred turn-of-the-century hunting, is correctly equated with Garrett Hardin's (1968) "tragedy of the commons." With the grazing commons owned by no one, all cattle owners have an incentive to add livestock to the pasture as long as valuable grass remains. Any individual who attempts to conserve the range will attract would-be grazers who can benefit by fattening their livestock. Similarly, the wildlife commons can result in a tragedy if the wildlife is unowned until killed. In the case of the bison, any hunter who decided to leave an animal to grow and reproduce would see the animal taken by the hunter over the rise. Indeed, the tragedy of the commons did occur.

From this tragedy, wildlife managers often draw the conclusion that markets and wildlife conservation are incompatible. Valerius Geist (1994, 492) is a leading spokesman for the proposition that "a global luxury market in wildlife is compatible with neither conservation nor good economics." Geist correctly asserts that "markets in dead wildlife reward its killing," but he incorrectly assumes that wildlife in their live state must remain in the commons. If there is no ownership of the live wild animals, markets will reward killing because no entrepreneur has the incentive to conserve the animals or their habitat. Indeed, if all grazing land was open to any grazer, it would be subject to tragedy. Hardin, however, also pointed out that private ownership of the resource in question can prevent the tragedy. Throughout most of the world, it is private property and fences that prevent this tragedy from occurring on grazing land.

Ownership of wildlife in the late nineteenth century was unlikely. Abundant stocks of wildlife made extinction appear impossible. Primitive fencing technology made the costs of fencing prohibitive, and ill-defined and enforced property rights to land made it difficult for an individual owner to control sufficient wildlife habitat to make a difference with management. For example, homestead laws limited ownership to 640 acres, hardly enough for effective habitat control. Without ownership of the land, ownership of the wildlife until it was killed was virtually impossible.

The wanton slaughter by turn-of-the-century market hunters left an institutional legacy that thwarts enviro-capitalism as it might be applied to wildlife today. State ownership dominates wildlife law. As a result, state wildlife authorities are quite proprietary in their approach to wildlife management. This attitude makes it difficult for private interests to take an active role in wildlife management. Further complicating market approaches to wildlife management is a democratic ideal rooted in opposition to the hunting privileges accorded nobility in England prior to the Magna Carta. The Crown's claim to wildlife limited public access to England's deer and game birds so that only the nobility and their friends could enjoy these fruits of the land. The establishment of limits on the Crown under the Magna Carta also guaranteed public access to wild game, and this aspect of English common law carried over to the new colonies and eventually the states. As a result, most hunters and anglers feel they have a democratic right to hunt and fish without paying a fee and perhaps without even having to ask permission. The combination of public ownership of wildlife and public ownership of land, especially in the western United States, makes it difficult for wildlife entrepreneurs to harness the forces of enviro-capitalism.

Many wildlife biologists actively oppose private wildlife management. For example, Valerius Geist (1994, 492) laments the fact that "the sorcerer's apprentice [markets] is already on the loose in several Canadian provinces and American states, where the rush toward game ranching has gutted wildlife conservation legislation, despite much adverse publicity and—largely futile—public opposition to powerful private interests." Such conclusions seem in keeping with Aldo Leopold's conclusion that game ranching is "undemocratic, unsocial, and therefore dangerous" (Leopold 1991c, 66). On the other hand, Leopold seemed to recognize the practicality of fee-based hunting when he argued that there was no need to reject market forces simply because "such tools are impure and unholy" (Leopold 1991a, 166). Leopold understood the importance of incentives for the landowner and asked whether there was any way "to induce the average farmer to leave the birds some food and cover without paying him for it?"

Wildlife in the Marketplace

Where profits can be made, however, it is difficult to keep Adam Smith's "invisible hand" from nudging us toward wildlife markets. Consider the government statistics on the demand for wildlife recreation in the United States (U.S. Department of the Interior 1993). In 1991, 14,063,000 hunters sixteen years old or older took to the field in the United States. Each spent an average of $984 per year in 1995 dollars. That works out to $12,336,000,000! Overall, hunters, anglers, hikers, birdwatchers, and other wildlife enthusiasts spent just over $67 billion in 1991 in pursuit of wildlife recreation. Expenditures included travel, lodging, equipment, licenses, user fees, membership dues—and land leasing and ownership.

Indeed, in 1991 alone, 1.5 million hunters and anglers spent $5.27 billion to purchase and $528.5 million to lease land for the primary purpose of fishing and hunting. Coupled with previous land purchases, hunters and anglers actually own approximately 19.5 million acres, equivalent to nearly nine Yellowstone Parks, for the primary purpose of hunting and fishing. Another 239 million acres have been leased by hunters and anglers, which is equivalent to the total acreage of all the national forests and national parks in the lower forty-eight states and then some. These figures, combined with the fact that 77 percent of all hunter-days took place on private lands, signal to entrepreneurs that profits can be made in wildlife habitat.

That signal is becoming stronger, too. In south central Texas, for example, landowners actually earn more from deer hunting operations than from cattle ranching. Dr. Will Cohen, a wildlife specialist for Texas A&M University, found this to be the case after studying sixty ranches in the region. He reports, "on some ranches, quail hunting reaps a higher return than either deer hunting or cattle ranching."[1] In addition, some state wildlife agencies are waking up to the opportunities in wildlife markets, even though this remains the exception. Wildlife officials at the Montana Department of Fish, Wildlife, and Parks, for instance, instituted a block management program for hunters near the end of the 1980s, whereby the state contracts with ranchers and farmers to provide controlled access for the hunting public. A limited number of hunters are allowed on each property on a given day, and they must adhere to landowner rules covering such things as registration and road use. In return, the state compensates landowners modestly with payments for crops and forage lost due to wildlife and helps landowners enforce rules of access. The program has worked so well for landowners and sportsmen that plans are now under way to up the ante to increase hunting opportunities on private lands. Among the changes, each landowner will get as much as $5,000 to participate in the block management program, with the funds coming from slightly higher license fees. The state's task force in charge of the new plan believes this will open more opportunities for hunters and send a stronger message to landowners that wildlife means profits.

Wildlife officials with the Texas Parks and Wildlife Department see new nongame market opportunities in birdwatching. Surveys show that the "Texas Hill Country" near the Gulf has become a mecca for birdwatchers and an economic boom for local communities.[2] For example, a 1990 survey showed that 1,485 members of the American Birding Association, one of several national birdwatching associations, spent a total of $5,009,914 that year visiting public and private birding sites along the Texas coast. Travel and tour spending claimed most of this, at $3,731,195. A 1991 survey of whooping crane tours near Rockport, Texas, showed that 15,561 birders participated in the tours, spending, on average, $200 per person. According to Diane Probst, executive director of the Rockport-Fulton Chamber of Commerce, "People from all over Texas and the U.S. come in big numbers and fill our shops and other attractions, as well as hotels, restaurants, and cities."[3] A number of Texas ranches and even state parks are tapping into this market by offering birdwatching tours, usually packaged with other recreational services. On the 825,000-acre King Ranch near Kingsville, daily tours include birdwatching and other wildlife viewing at different sites on the ranch. The daily tours cost $40 per person and last four to five hours. A special full-day combined birdwatching and wildlife tour, lunch included, is available for $100 per person.[4]

Hunters, anglers, birdwatchers, and other wildlife enthusiasts who understand Leopold's nexus between landowner incentives and wild-life habitat have provided the demand side of wildlife preservation, but it takes entrepreneurs to provide the supply. As the following stories show, both not-for-profit and for-profit firms are being established to fill the void where wildlife opportunities on public lands are poor and deteriorating, or nonexistent.

Two in the Bush

The zebra cautiously approached the water hole, unaware of the danger perched in the tree above. African animals are conditioned to be cautious by predators that make life precarious, but in this case, the predator was well concealed. As the zebra lowered his head to drink, the archer, stiff from hours of sitting patiently in the tree stand, drew his powerful bow and launched the razor-sharp arrow. Instantly, the zebra fell to the ground as the arrow severed his spinal cord. The meat would become dog food because humans generally find it inedible, but the tanned zebra skin would decorate the floor of the hunter's trophy room.

To the nonhunter this crass "slaughter" of a magnificent African animal for pure human pleasure engenders feelings of disgust and anger sufficient to mobilize antihunting forces. Killing for meat might be rationalized, but killing strictly for pleasure is not to be tolerated. Accordingly, antihunting forces believe that laws should be passed to protect innocent animals from human self-aggrandizement. With the individual animal as the focal point, the killing of the zebra or any other animal is seen simply as a merciless act that decreases wildlife populations for human pleasure.

But the focus on the individual animal is misplaced if we are truly concerned with biodiversity and survival of species, because such a focus fails to ask what can be done to preserve habitat and ensure a sustainable animal population in the future. Every hunter experiences a moment of remorse for the individual animal at the time of the kill, but most understand their role in a larger scheme of wildlife management. Indeed, it is often only the hunter who is a spokesman, in the political process or in the private sector, for wildlife. "The rest of the story" of the zebra kill described above reveals the role of the hunter, the entrepreneur, and profits in South African game preservation.

Angus Brown and his partner Clive Perkins are professional hunters and enviro-capitalists motivated by both their love of the bush and the profits that they can make from good resource stewardship. The two have contracted with Piet Lamprecht, the owner of approximately 20,000 acres in the northern Transvaal province of South Africa. According to their contract, Angus Brown Safaris provides the accommodations and guide services while Lamprecht provides the habitat. In this case the accommodations include beautiful African huts with walls woven from reeds and roofs thatched from grass. Horns from animals indigenous to the area adorn the walls and skins cover the floors. Food in the camp is typical South African fare, highlighted by the wild meat killed by the hunters. Natural pans and developed water holes (bore holes, as South Africans call them) provide water for the animals in this arid land on the edge of the Kalahari Desert. At these water points, archery hunters sit in tree stands or ground blinds waiting for animals such as the zebra to come for their daily drink. All of these capital improvements are possible only because hunters are willing to pay a fee for the services.

Perhaps more important, however, is the impact that hunting revenues have on land management. As the landowner, Lamprecht gets a share of the daily hunting fees paid by the customers as well as two-thirds of the trophy fees paid for each animal. The remainder of the fees go to Brown and Perkins. These fees provide the incentive to carefully manage wildlife and its habitat, for unlike most hunting in North America where the license fees generally go to state or federal agencies, trophy fees in South Africa go to the people who have the largest stake in good wildlife management. Like a menu at a restaurant, a price list goes to the hunter: tsessebe $1,500; zebra $750; kudu $700; wildebeest $700; blesbok $250; warthog $100; impala $80; and the list goes on. Brown, Perkins, and Lamprecht mutually set the prices to reflect the relative scarcity of the species. With warthogs and impala abundant, prices are low; with tsessebe and waterbuck scarce in the region, prices are high.

What impact do these fees have? On the demand side, the hunter facing a budget constraint must carefully weigh preferences against price. Hunters might think a tsessebe would make a nice addition to the trophy room, but the price of $1,500 translates into two or three of the less scarce big animals, such as zebra or kudu. Indeed, though not on Lamprecht's property, Angus Brown Safaris can arrange hunting for elephant or rhino, the two most scarce of the hunted species, at a price of $12,000 and $28,000, respectively. Needless to say, this reduces the quantity demanded by pricing most hunters out of the market.

These fees can be charged because South African game laws give ownership of wildlife to the landowner who fences his property with game-proof fences. Approximately ten feet high with fifteen to twenty strands of tightly stretched smooth-steel wire, these fences halt the migration of most animals from one property to the next. Like cattle, the wildlife become private property to be husbanded. While this may take some of the "wildness" out of the hunting experience, it is not like hunting in a small pasture; 20,000 acres gives the animals plenty of habitat and escape routes in the thick bush.

The supply-side impact of these incentives is dramatic. Piet Lamprecht's ranch used to be mainly a cattle operation with some cultivated fields of peanuts and cotton. The potential for hunting profits has changed this. The owner has removed all but a few cattle from the land. He is also removing interior fences necessary for cattle management to give wildlife a freer range, and water points are being converted from troughs to more natural water holes. Because of hunting revenues, instead of carrying several hundred Brahma cattle, the land supports approximately 500 impala, 150 kudu, 100 wildebeest, 150 gemsbok, 50 tsessebe, 50 waterbuck, and numerous other species. Brown, Perkins, and Lamprecht begin each hunting season by estimating the number of harvestable animals and agreeing on prices for each species. They consider ways to improve the habitat and whether it would be profitable to invest in importing other species, such as cape buffalo, indigenous to the region but now largely absent. Without the profits from hunting, less habitat would be available for the indigenous species of the Kalahari, and fewer animals would survive.

As enviro-capitalists, Angus Brown and Clive Perkins provide capital, contract with the other input owners, including the landowner, cooks, and trackers, and market the product to the hunters. And as result of this entrepreneurship, southern African animals and the people of the region have a better chance to survive and coexist. Well-known safari writer Peter Hathaway Capstick captures the important nexus.

The interesting thing is that untold hundreds of thousands of hectares and *morgen* that even a few years ago were scrub grazing for a mix of game and cattle have now been entirely allocated to game. Why? Economics, as always. Game pays its own way, eats nearly anything, is more resistant to disease and predators, and generally produces a higher and better use for the land. . . . Even the old enemies become assets to the farmer who switches from cattle to game. One friend of mine used to lose as many as thirty calves a season to leopards. . . . Now, those same leopards are worth a cool $1,000 to $1,500 [in 1995 the values would be $2,500 to $3,000] each to sport hunters, not a bad trade-off for animals that caused a liability of well over ten grand and had to be poisoned! Tell me, is that bad for leopards? (Capstick 1983, 18–19)

Bird and Breakfast Anyone?

Not far from Angus Brown's bush camp in the northern Natal province in South Africa, two other enviro-capitalists are capitalizing on smaller species. Not every hunter is interested in big game; many, especially Spaniards and Italians, care only about bird hunting. To accommodate them, William Whipp and Willem Koch are leasing bird-hunting rights on suitable properties. They work with the landowners to manage the habitat and increase the populations of natural game birds. As in the United States, farmers in the region had little reason to worry about protective cover until the birds became an asset. Now instead of minimizing costs by cropping large fields, the farmers leave cover strips between maizelands (corn in the United States) and refrain from harvesting some of the maize and sorghum to provide both cover and food for the birds. The populations of guinea fowl, francolin, and quail have mushroomed accordingly.

Trevor Couiens, a farmer on Blood River marsh in northern Natal, takes advantage of his waterfowl habitat. The marsh is a resting area for thousands of Egyptian geese, yellow-billed teal, red-billed teal, and Hottentot teal. Couiens set up feeding stations with blinds around the marsh and built a hunting camp. Hunts are sold to groups of four shotgunners per group at $200 per gun per day. Bag limits are set by the South African National Parks Board, which works closely with landowners like Couiens. A typical day finds the hunter in the blinds thirty minutes before sunrise to shoot waterfowl for two to three hours. Hunters return to camp for breakfast between 8:30 A.M. and 9:30 A.M., and then leave for three hours of hunting guinea fowl and francolin in the croplands. If hunters haven't had enough foot hunting, they can return to the fields for a couple more hours after a leisurely lunch. Then, it is back into the blinds for waterfowl until sunset. The business has been so successful that it is generally fully booked six months in advance.

As the bird-hunting business has grown, landowners are earning more from their lands, professional hunters are making a profit and employing the local people, and hunters are getting a quality experience. Perhaps more importantly, bird populations have grown tremendously, proving that hunting makes it is possible to do good while doing well.

Similar bird-hunting enterprise is occurring in the United States. In some cases, the farmer has turned wildlife entrepreneur. In Montana, wheat farmer Don Jenni found that there are enough pheasant hunters willing to pay $25 per day to hunt on his land that he is encouraging habitat for them. Strips of cover are left next to crops and ditch banks, and fence rows that used to be burned are not being disturbed. Farmers in North and South Dakota, Iowa, Nebraska, and Kansas are realizing profit from pheasant hunting as well. As a result, farmers are giving protection of pheasant higher priority on their lands. Other entrepreneurs are establishing hunting resorts. According to the 1994–1995 edition of the *Directory of Hunting Resorts*, 357 private hunting enterprises now operate in the United States, which represents a more than three-fold increase since the 1970s. Writing in the directory, John M. Mullin explains why these enterprises are growing:

> The old "law of supply and demand" is still working in favor of private enterprise hunting resorts. In most of the states where preserves are plentiful, there is a lack of so-called "open hunting" for upland game-birds. . . . As in everything else where the "product demand" exceeds the available supply, private enterprise eventually steps in to satisfy the demand. . . . It's a fact that there is now more wildlife habitat and "escape cover" on a good hunting resort than there is on a *hundred* average farms—after the crops are harvested. It's no wonder the preserve concept is *growing*! (Mullin N.d.)

MUM's the Word

Ten years ago, biologist Wayne Long started a wildlife consulting business to help farmers, ranchers, and other rural landowners turn their lands into productive wildlife habitat and achieve higher profits. Says Long, "It was slow at first, but today business is booming."[5]

Long circulates a newsletter to hundreds of clients and interested land managers who recognize the potential to harmonize wildlife management with good land stewardship. The headlines in his newsletter, *The Game Manager*, include "Mule Deer Population Decline & How We Can Stop It," "Improving Your Land for Turkeys," and "Brush Management Colorado Style." His pitch for the services of his firm states that almost any ranch or farm can benefit from a wildlife management plan. His firm's specialty is integrating traditional livestock and farming practices with wildlife concerns to increase profits. Given that his firm's list of clients has more than tripled in the last four years, he must be doing just that.

How did Wayne Long get into this innovative business? While studying wildlife management at Utah State University, Long recognized that his course of studies focused entirely on the wildlife and not at all on their habitat. Working for the California Department of Fish and Game made him realize why studying habitat management was irrelevant to public wildlife managers; they have no control over it. A huge chunk of public land is controlled by agencies separate from the wildlife agencies, and private lands are just that, private. In short, public wildlife managers mainly set seasons, bag limits, and license fees and enforce the rules for taking wildlife. With rare exceptions, they cannot manage the habitat.

Long realized that proper management of wildlife required management of the habitat itself. But how could this happen when most of the high-quality wildlife habitat is in other people's hands? Like many other wildlife entrepreneurs, Long found opportunities for managing the habitat and developing new ways for making wildlife pay.

In 1962, Long started his career as wildlife entrepreneur when he became manager of the Dye Creek Preserve, a 37,000-acre property in central California. Interestingly the Dye Creek Preserve is leased from its owner, the state of California, by the Nature Conservancy, an environmental organization dedicated to preservation of endangered species and their habitat. To finance management of the land, the conservancy has conducted a fee-hunting program at Dye Creek for twenty-five years. The fee schedule for 1995–96 included season deer hunting privileges at $700, season waterfowl memberships at $600, two-day guided pig hunts at $625, and guided turkey hunts at $300 per day. Under the active direction of Long and his firm, Multiple Use Managers (MUM), the Dye Creek Preserve sustains healthy populations of wild boar, deer, wild turkey, dove, and quail, and hosts abundant numbers of migrating waterfowl. Deer hunters at Dye Creek enjoy success rates of 75 percent compared to the California state average of 10 percent.

Active hunting management is only one approach used by MUM on Dye Creek. To capitalize on a growing demand for nonconsumptive use of wildlife, MUM also offers guided photographic safaris and provides accommodations at a lodge on the property. And the Nature

Conservancy itself participates in the production side of Dye Creek's amenities by offering educational field trips for its members.

Of course, the conservancy is interested in more than revenues generated from hunting and other activities; its primary mission is to preserve rare habitat and enhance species diversity. At Dye Creek, the approach is showing noticeable results. Once scarce or absent black bears, mountain lions, otters, beavers, eagles, and vultures now thrive on the preserve.

Like many young businesses, MUM had its growing pains. Initially Long had a difficult time finding clients, but a growing demand for hunting combined with MUM's success at Dye Creek have enabled Long to expand his business. Today Long and his son, along with four full-time employees and four seasonal employees, manage 600,000 acres of private land in five states (California, Colorado, Montana, New Mexico, and Alaska). Two of MUM's properties are exclusively wildlife ranches, but most of their ranches integrate wildlife management into traditional livestock and timber operations.

In addition to managing private wildlife lands, MUM appraises land for wildlife potential and brokers deals for people interested in acquiring wildlife properties for their own use or as investments. Just as duck hunting clubs flourished in the 1970s, big-game hunting preserves became popular in the 1980s and 1990s.

MUM supervises hunting on Santa Rosa Island, one of the islands in the Channel Island National Park. Off the coast of California, the 54,000-acre island is home to approximately 1,200 Roosevelt elk and 1,000 mule deer transplanted there between 1910 and 1920. To keep the elk and deer from overgrazing the habitat, the Vail & Vichens Cattle Co., the prior owner and now lessee, employs MUM to manage an annual hunt. In 1996 the hunters shot thirty bull elk. If they are on the island for an elk hunt, hunters pay $7,500 for a four-day trophy elk hunt; other hunters pay $3,500 for a four-day mule deer hunt, or a $2,500 trophy fee for deer.

Due to the destructive nature of the wild pigs that roamed the island for well over 100 years, the National Park Service contracted with MUM in 1991 to eradicate the pigs. MUM accomplished this during an eleven-month operation. Over 1,000 pigs were removed using helicopter shooting and trapping and ground hunting with dogs.

Ted and Jane's Place

Media mogul Ted Turner and his wife, Jane Fonda, have gotten into the wildlife business, too, for both profit and pleasure. Their Flying D

Ranch in southwest Montana encompasses 107,514 deeded acres of steep Douglas fir forests, rolling grass hills, and meadowed stream bottoms. The land was a working cattle ranch until 1989 when Turner purchased it. In return for valuable tax deductions, Turner Enterprises granted conservation easements to the Nature Conservancy, removed the cattle, improved the fences, and converted the Flying D to a bison ranch. By 1993 the ranch was stocked with 3,391 bison raised mainly to stock his other bison ranches. The ranch also provides excellent wildlife habitat, especially for elk and deer, and the streams on the property offer fine trout fishing. Golden and bald eagles soar overhead, and occasionally grizzly bears, bighorn sheep, and mountain goats pass through.

The previous owner, Shelton Ranches, recognized the rising value of the wildlife assets in the 1980s and began actively restricting access and managing for trophy elk. The impact of this management has been dramatic. Since 1981, the elk population has grown from 757 to 3,163 in 1996—a 420 percent increase! During the same period, elk herds generally increased in Montana, but by far less. The increase on the Flying D was achieved by restricting the number and size of bulls harvested and by increasing the harvest of cow elk, thus reducing the cow-to-bull ratio. As a result, calf crops generally run 50 to 60 percent and immature bulls (those with fewer than five points on each antler) are numerous. General manager Russ Miller employs a professional hunting guide, Rob Arnaud, who looks after the hunting operation. They use a helicopter, fixed-wing aircraft, and observations by ranch employees to establish an extensive data base on wildlife populations. Their annual wildlife report provides Miller, Arnaud, and state wildlife officials with data on herd size, harvest data, and age and sex, all necessary to control the number and type of elk harvested each year.

Miller himself is not a hunter, so as general manager, he sees the wildlife as competitors with his main crop, bison. Given that elk consume grass that bison could be eating, Miller is attempting to make the elk to pay their way. The Flying D's week-long guided elk hunts sell for $9,500 (not including state license fees), and in 1996 his thirty elk hunters harvested twenty-eight trophy bulls. The elk hunters were also allowed to hunt mule and white-tailed deer and, if successful, were charged additional trophy fees of $3,500 and $2,500, respectively. To help cull old bulls from the herd, hunters can shoot a bison bull on the Flying D. In 1996, twelve hunters did so, at a price of $3,500 each.

Producing gross revenues of approximately $300,000, wildlife on the Flying D is an asset.[6] Wildlife is producing income for the ranching enterprise, employment for the guides, and quality trophy hunts for the clients. The public also benefits from Turner's wildlife management. Abundant herds spill over onto adjacent public lands where access is unrestricted. Moreover, to keep the sex distribution of the herd in balance, Miller and Arnaud work with the Montana Department of Fish, Wildlife, and Parks and allow free access to the Flying D for restricted public hunting of cow elk. As one Montana rancher puts it, "If it pays, it stays." Wildlife is likely to stay on the Flying D.

City Slickers

A couple of third-generation Montana boys, Ted and John Flynn, have gotten into the fee-recreation business, too, on a smaller scale. The brothers, who live on their family cattle ranch near Townsend, know every inch of their domain but not necessarily because they spend hours on horseback herding cattle from pasture to pasture. Much of their knowledge of the land comes from countless hours spent hunting. In fact, it might be fair to say that cattle ranching is just a sideline that pays the bills so they can pursue their hunting passion. During the hunting season, the Flynn brothers can usually be found at the cabin their grandfather built on the banks of Dry Creek. Here, like their father and grandfather before them, they have joined friends for years to share hunting stories around the warm stove.

In the "good old days," hunters from this cabin could range for miles in any direction without seeing other people or worrying about trespassing. In the 1980s, however, this began to change. Hassled by increasing hunting pressure, landowners began to restrict access to their private lands. Big spreads were purchased by out-of-state interests who often restricted access. For example, the neighboring Bar-None Ranch, comprising 21,315 acres and home to an estimated 430 elk, is now part of Ted Turner's hunting operation. With increasing hunting pressure, even the smaller, local landowners began restricting access to private lands. Before, with only a few hunters seeking access, landowners could be neighborly and provide a free lunch, but population and hunting pressure were increasing the cost to the landowner of providing that lunch.

Facing more restrictions on access, the Flynn brothers and their friends had to adjust if they wanted to maintain a quality hunting experience. Of course, they could always hunt on their own land, but hunting big game requires larger tracts, especially for elk, which can migrate over vast territories. Unlike the Flying D Ranch, which is one contiguous ownership unit, land ownership around the Flynn Ranch is fragmented, ranging from small cabin sites to parcels of thousands of acres. Also, unlike the hunting clients on the Flying D, the Flynns and their friends were not wealthy hunters who could pay $9,500 per year for an elk hunt.

Obtaining access to the land in fragmented ownership at a reasonable price required entrepreneurship, of which the Flynns have much. In 1987, they solved the problem by establishing Greyson Creek Meadows Recreation, Inc., a corporation that enters into leases with local ranchers. According to the leases, Greyson Creek pays a fee for access and in some cases an additional fee if animals are harvested on the property, posts and patrols the land against trespass, carries liability insurance, and agrees to abide by several other rules, including only driving on the properties to retrieve game or get to cabin sites. For the landowner, this lease arrangement removes most of the hassles associated with managing hunters, and it provides additional income. Through these leases, Greyson Creek pays annual lease fees of approximately $15,000 and controls access to approximately 30,000 acres of private land, including the Flynn Ranch.

Members of the Greyson Creek corporation pay an annual fee of $450 for individuals and $500 for families, much less than they might pay for a membership at a country club or a season pass at a ski resort. In return for this fee, the thirty-five to forty Greyson Creek members receive access to the leased lands and use of three cabins for year-round recreation. Hunting pressure is much less than on open access public lands, which improves the hunting experience. In addition to members, the Flynns guide nonmembers for a fee, thus adding to the revenues of Greyson Creek Meadows Recreation, Inc.

While not as productive as large, contiguous properties like the Flying D, the Greyson Creek properties still have abundant elk and deer and increasing populations of black bears, mountain lions, coyotes, and eagles. With vehicular access restricted, both game and nongame species are being found in areas where, previously, too much human pressure kept them away. Members are encouraged to harvest the more mature elk and deer so as to improve the quality of the herds. The Flynns are cutting some timber on their property, but they are doing so selectively. Their careful logging practices open up the forest floor to provide more forage for both cattle and wildlife but leave sufficient cover for protection from the weather and escape from hunters. While there are no annual game censuses, Greyson Creek members agree that the restricted access and more systematic management of the properties have increased the number of species they see and improved the quality of the recreation experience.

The Flynns' entrepreneurial radars continue beyond the establishment of Greyson Creek, scanning the horizon for other profit opportunities that can sustain their ranching lifestyle. Montana High Country Cattle Drives is another profitable enterprise that depends on the environmental amenities on the Flynn Ranch. Recognizing a growing recreational demand from nonhunters, the brothers established a week-long cattle drive that gives city slickers an opportunity to enjoy the romantic Old West. Guests pay $1,500 to ride horses, move cattle from one pasture to another, and enjoy the atmosphere of a campfire and chuckwagon at the end of a day's work. Horses, gear, and expertise are provided by several of the Flynns' friends who have outfitting businesses that usually focus on hunting and fishing. In June, however, the demand for these activities is low, so the cattle drive provides an opportunity to get some use and profit out of horses and pack gear. Guests are attracted by the romantic image of the western cowboy, but they would not find the experience as valuable were it not for the clean air and water, abundant wildlife, and beautiful scenery. As John Flynn put it, "We are in the business of processing sunlight, water, and grass, and it doesn't matter whether the waste [not quite his word] comes from the end of a cow or an elk."

Simonds Says . . .

No discussion of fee hunting would be complete without a discussion of Utah's Deseret Ranch and the enviro-capitalist who made the ranch a showcase of environmental innovation. Gregg Simonds is the entrepreneur who made this possible. He describes himself as a man who was long on ideas but short on experience when he started working for Deseret Land & Livestock Company, first in the early 1980s as a consultant for its farming and wildlife operations and later as the ranch's general manager. Simonds's ideas came from his graduate studies in range science at Utah State University and from the teachings of Allen Savory, a range specialist noted for his "holistic resource management" approach. According to this approach, cattle are not merely consumers of grass, they are management tools to improve the health of the range. To be sure, not all ranchers accept the holistic resource management approach. But it does work for entrepreneurs like

Simonds, whose innovative ideas on farming, ranching, and wildlife management operations have transformed the Deseret Ranch into a place where profits, wildlife, and cattle production coexist.

The ranch comprises 201,000 acres in Utah and Wyoming. Approximately 7,500 acres are irrigated, and additional federal land is leased for grazing. The elevation of the ranch ranges from 6,000 to over 8,500 feet. Vegetative types vary from sagebrush and grassland to mountain forests.

Deseret is a study in contrasts. This ranch is different from most in the region and not only because it is owned by the Church of Jesus Christ of Latter-Day Saints (the Mormon church). Simonds manages livestock with a concern for its impact on wildlife and the land; he addresses production problems with ingenuity and the help of nature rather than with expensive machinery and human toil. At Deseret, the combination of more cattle, more bison, more elk, and more deer has translated into a healthier bottom line simply because Simonds and his operations' managers were able to improve range productivity, lower cattle feeding costs, and increase ranch revenues through fee hunting. The purpose of the ranch is to make a profit, while at the same time, improving the land, water, and wildlife resources and sharing the knowledge with others in the process.

Attention to wildlife management began in 1976 and was enhanced in 1982 when wildlife biologist Shane Davis came to work at Deseret. As manager of wildlife operations, Davis's objective was "to maintain a healthy, balanced, free-ranging, self-sufficient wildlife population" and "to show that wildlife and livestock can coexist on the range and benefit each other" (quoted in McCutcheon 1987). He was able to meet these objectives largely through the profits generated from fee hunting. Indeed, the fee-hunting arm of the wildlife operation has proved most lucrative at Deseret, generating from 25 to 50 percent of the ranch's net profit each year, depending on the price of cattle. Simonds says the wildlife enterprise at Deseret "made us more balanced resource managers. . . . We have become more committed to the fact that wildlife is an important part of the land resource model: we want to preserve, protect, and enhance this resource for its benefit, ours, and the public's" (Simonds 1988).

The ranch supports wildlife populations of 2,000 elk, 5,000 mule deer, 500 antelope, and 50–100 moose. Since 1976, elk numbers have increased from 350 to 2,000, and reproductive rates are now 65 percent (compared with 55 percent on neighboring lands and 17 percent in Yellowstone National Park). Nongame species also have benefited indirectly by the increased sensitivity to big-game production. Surveys show that there is an increasing presence of squirrels, jack rabbits, beavers, minks, mountain lions, cougars, and black bears. Raptor nest sites (including bald and gold eagles) are inventoried, as are populations of other birds residing on the ranch, such as cormorants, egrets, terns, and sage grouses. Beavers have been introduced on the ranch to stabilize water flows. In areas where the beavers have not stayed, Deseret's wildlife biologists have mimicked them by building small dams to help catch silt and stabilize stream banks. Ranch biologists have also planted willow shoots to help these plants become reestablished in riparian areas.

The ranch's wildlife operation derives all of its income from hunting fees, but they have plans to branch out into nonconsumptive wildlife use. Approximately 1,500 vehicles pass the ranch each day, and many of the drivers stop to view the elk grazing in the winter. A joint program for viewing wildlife for a fee is being planned with the Bureau of Land Management and the state of Utah, whereby the bureau will provide a site for parking, the state will provide the signs, and the ranch will erect fences and patrol the viewing area. In addition, the ranch is planning to operate wildlife workshops and is investigating the possibility of opening a visitors' center.

Cattle are still the mainstay of the ranch's business, but it is how the cattle are managed for the benefit of land that is entrepreneurial. One of the most important tools here is the ranch's grazing plan, described by Bill Hopkin, manager of cattle operations, as a "biological plan to budget our grass and improve the land resource." The secret is in the ranch's grazing techniques during the rapid growing season for grasses and forage plants in early May to late June. "By limiting the amount of time the cattle stay in a pasture, an average of five days during the rapid growing season, wanted plants are not damaged, can actually benefit from cropping by the cattle—and have the chance to grow. By winter, the ranch's lower pastures have recovered and are able to sustain the cattle through the winter" (McCutcheon 1987). Moving thousands of cattle after short periods of time could be quite labor intensive, but at Deseret imagination solved the problem. Hopkin says, "We move them with a police siren on a pickup instead of pushing them. We've tried to teach them [the cattle] that when they hear the siren, they can go through the gate to a fresh pasture. The best reward of all is a fresh, green, lush pasture" (quoted in McCutcheon 1987).

There is plenty of enthusiasm at Deseret, as well there should. To Simonds and his compadres, all full of unconventional ideas, the ranch became a proving ground for the unconventional—a dream come true. Indeed, at Deseret tradition took a back seat, and wildlife and cattle prosper together.

Public Game, Private Profit

A stumbling block to successful wildlife entrepreneurship in the United States has been that wildlife itself is owned by the state, and harvests are strictly controlled by state agencies. Coupled with this is the fact that most hunters in the West associate hunting with public lands where access is free. As Dwight Schuh (1990, 105) puts it in *Sports Afield*, "In eleven western states there are huge areas of federal land available to everyone." He asserts that hunting there is "hassle-free" but acknowledges that game is often hard to find and that beating the competition to what game there is challenges the public land hunter.

Old traditions die hard, however, and hunters, having become accustomed to free hunting on both private and public domain, balk at paying for access. Indeed, they openly oppose introducing markets into wildlife allocation citing "market hunting" in the late nineteenth century as the cause of declining wildlife populations. By continually making it more difficult for landowners to profit from wildlife, encouraging open access to the animals, and pricing hunting licenses below their market value, these market opponents perpetuate equal access to an increasingly lower quality hunting experience. Moreover, by making it difficult for the landowner to profit from providing habitat, opponents of market hunting take away the crucial incentive recognized in 1930 by the American Game Policy Committee, chaired by Aldo Leopold. As Leopold (1991b, 152) put it, "Compensate him [the landowner] directly or indirectly for producing a game crop and for the privilege of harvesting it." As examples above illustrate, however, opposition does not repress the entrepreneurial spirit, especially where there is a demand for quality hunting and fishing experiences. These entrepreneurs discovered how to control access and devise innovative contractual arrangements to capture a share of the hunting and fishing profits. When they are successful, "the tragedy of the commons" associated with wildlife management is mitigated.

The results of a hunter survey conducted by Robert Davis of the University of Colorado are informative. In 1991 Davis surveyed forty-nine western Colorado big-game hunters, fifteen of whom paid a fee for access. His results are reported in tables 4.1 and 4.2. The quality factors

TABLE 4.1
Scores of Quality Factors, Fee and Non-Fee Hunters
N (Fees) = 14, N (Non-fees) = 35

Variable	Pay Fees	Pay No Fees	Significance Level*
Seeing Game	86.5	70.5	0.0015
Less Crowding	84.5	66.6	0.0040
Easy Access	75.0	50.3	0.0800
Total Quality	83.4	77.0	0.0900

*Based on *t* test of difference between means.
Source: Davis (1995, 115). Table 4.1 is reprinted with permission of Rowman & Littlefield Publishers, Inc.

TABLE 4.2
Scores of Quality Factors: Public and Private Land Hunters
N (Public) = 24, N (Private) = 25

Variable	Public Land	Private Land	Significance Level*
Lack of Crowding	63.4	81.7	0.01
Seeing Game	70.5	80.9	0.03
Total Quality	74.9	82.0	0.03
Ease of Access	47.8	70.7	0.08

*Based on *t* test of difference between means.
Source: Davis (1995, 115). Table 4.2 is reprinted with permission of Rowman & Littlefield Publishers, Inc.

that seem most important are the likelihood of seeing game and the likelihood of not seeing other hunters. Hunters who paid a fee for access to private land were more satisfied with the amount of game they saw, the reduced crowding, and even the ease of access. Comparing the quality of hunting experiences on public and private land revealed similar results. Hunters on public land saw less game, encountered more hunters, and had to work harder for access. Davis concludes,

"The differences reflect the positive experiences reported by fee paying hunters and the negative effects of uncontrolled access on the quality of hunting" (Davis 1995, 116).

From Africa to Colorado, markets are making their way into hunting because entrepreneurs are meeting a demand. In the process, both the hunters and the habitat owners profit. The nonhunter may think that the wildlife themselves are left out of the transaction. To be sure, it is the killing of animals that generates the profits, but it is also this killing that provides the incentive to people to preserve habitat and species. Russell Taylor, an ecologist with the World Wildlife Fund in Zimbabwe, captures the important difference between the view of the conservationist-hunter and the animal rights supporter: "The animal rights people want to save individual animals. As a biologist, I want to save populations" (quoted in Bonner 1993, 265).

Like entrepreneurs in conventional economic endeavors, wildlife entrepreneurs must understand the complexities of production and marketing. On the production side, wildlife entrepreneurs have been busy finding innovative ways in which wildlife can compete effectively with other traditional land uses, such as cattle ranching or farming. Because of Angus Brown's and Clive Perkins's efforts to produce a high-quality product, Piet Lamprecht, the landowner with whom they contract for hunting territory, realized that there were higher rewards from wildlife production. By cutting back on the number of cattle grazing on his land, Lamprecht could produce more African wildlife.

Entrepreneurship means that there will be a multitude of approaches to production. The approach taken by Angus Brown Safaris will not work for everyone. Unlike so much public wildlife management, where production is based on a "one-size-fits-all" approach, approaches vary, depending on the circumstances of time and place and the ingenuity of the entrepreneur. Gregg Simonds on the Deseret Ranch believed he did not have to give up cattle production to get more wildlife. By implementing a unique grazing rotation plan and utilizing the natural water supplies, he was able to increase both cattle and elk numbers on his ranch.

As with other economic goods and services, however, raw inputs often require entrepreneurial talent to transform them into products valued highly by consumers. Wildlife habitat is the raw input being produced by Angus Brown Safaris and Deseret Ranch, but the final product is a unique hunting experience. The Flynn brothers see themselves of processors of sunshine, water, and grass to produce cattle and wildlife. Their traditional output, cattle, is sold through well-established markets, but they had to work hard at packaging and marketing the amenity values. Throughout Montana are many ranches with the same inputs, but it takes entrepreneurship to market these assets to consumers.

Because these enviro-capitalists reap the rewards of their production and marketing innovations, entrepreneurship is switched on. The Flynn brothers enjoy higher returns from their ranch because of their entrepreneurship. In Mississippi, a 10,000-acre tract leased for hunting generates $10 per acre, returning $100,000 annually. Using a discount rate of 10 percent, this means that hunting increases the value of the property by $1 million (Shelton 1990, 261). This kind of return gets the attention of landowners.

Switching on entrepreneurship in the public sector is harder but not impossible, as we shall see in chapter 9. Driven by budgets that depend on hunter satisfaction, some state fish and game departments are beginning to realize the importance of private land in the production process. In states such as New Mexico, California, and Colorado, public employees with vision in these agencies are instituting new programs that allow private landowners to capitalize on wildlife assets by granting them special permits and more flexibility in hunting regulations. Everyone—hunters, landowners, wildlife managers, and even the wildlife—wins when this entrepreneurial approach is used.

Challenges remain for the wildlife entrepreneur, especially when the wildlife is migratory and crosses political boundaries. But where there is a will, there is a way, as we saw from the Adopt a Pothole program discussed in chapter 3. Entrepreneurs are experimenting with compensation schemes for landowners who allow predators such as wolves and grizzly bears access to their land. For example, Hank Fischer, the Northern Rockies director of Defenders of Wildlife, used his entrepreneurial talents to raise funds to compensate livestock owners for wolf depredation and to reward private landowners who allow wolves to raise pups on their property.

In addition to production and marketing constraints, entrepreneurs face institutional constraints that often thwart their innovations. Laws that do not include water used to enhance instream flows as a "beneficial use," requirements that private landowners must allow public access, and restrictions on the sale of wildlife for profit stymie entrepreneurship. Removing such constraints allows entrepreneurs to experiment with a whole host of wildlife management approaches.

Notes

1. Telephone interview with Dr. Will Cohen, wildlife specialist for the Texas A&M University Research and Extension, 27 December 1993.
2. Data provided by Texas Parks and Wildlife Department, Nongame & Urban Wildlife Branch, Austin, Texas.
3. Quoted in an undated news release issued by the Rockport-Fulton Area (Texas) Chamber of Commerce, "Hummer/Bird Celebration 1994."
4. Data provided by King Ranch Visitor Center, Kingsville, Texas.
5. Telephone interview with Wayne Long, 5 January 1996.
6. We estimate this on the basis of data in the ranch's annual wildlife report.

References

Bonner, Raymond. 1993. *At the Hand of Man: Peril and Hope for Africa's Wildlife*. New York: Knopf.

Capstick, Peter Hathaway. 1983. *Safari: The Last Adventure*. New York: St. Martin's Press.

Davis, Robert K. 1995. A New Paradigm in Wildlife Conservation: Using Markets to Produce Big Game Hunting. In *Wildlife in the Marketplace*, ed. Terry L. Anderson and Peter J. Hill. Lanham, MD: Rowman and Littlefield Publishers, 107–25.

Geist, Valerius. 1994. Wildlife Conservation as Wealth. *Nature*, April 7.

Hardin, Garrett. 1968. Tragedy of the Commons. *Science* 162: 1243–48.

Leopold, Aldo. 1991a. Game and Wild Life Conservation [1932]. In *The River of the Mother of God and Other Essays by Aldo Leopold*, ed. Susan L. Flader and J. Baird Callicott. Madison: University of Wisconsin Press, 164–68.

———. 1991b. Report to the American Game Conference on an American Game Policy [1930]. In *The River of the Mother of God and Other Essays by Aldo Leopold*, ed. Susan L. Flader and J. Baird Callicott. Madison: University of Wisconsin Press, 150–55.

———. 1991c. Wild Lifers vs. Game Farmers: A Plea for Democracy in Sport [1919]. In *The River of the Mother of God and Other Essays by Aldo Leopold*, ed. Susan L. Flader and J. Baird Callicott. Madison: University of Wisconsin Press, 62–70.

McCutcheon, Pat. 1987. Deseret—Doing More With Less. *Herald Journal/Cache Sunday*, June 21.

Mullin, John M. N.d. Why Is the Preserve Concept Growing? In *Directory of Hunting Resorts*, 1994–1995 ed., comp./ed. Peggy Mullin Buehmer. Goose Lake, IA: Wildlife Harvest Publications.

Schuh, Dwight. 1990. American Hunting Heritage. *Sports Afield*, February.

Shelton, Ross, III. 1990. Stewardship for Profit: Dollars and Cents. In *Conference Proceedings: Income Opportunities for the Private Landowner through Manage-*

ment of Natural Resources and Recreational Access, ed. William N. Grafton et al. Morgantown: West Virginia University Extension Service, 258–63.

Simonds, Gregg. 1988. How Incentives Affect Resource Management on a Western Ranch. Presentation given at National Conference for Journalists, Big Sky, Montana, sponsored by the Political Economy Research Center, Sept. 7–11.

U.S. Department of the Interior, Fish and Wildlife Service and U.S. Department of Commerce, Bureau of the Census. 1993. *1991 National Survey of Fishing, Hunting, and Wildlife-Associated Recreation*. Washington, DC: U.S. Government Printing Office.

Chapter 5

Buy That Fish a Drink

. . . trying to rehabilitate the environment means recognizing all
water interests.

—Zach Willey
Environmental Defense Fund

If you tried to cross Montana's Gallatin River, a blue-ribbon trout
stream with its source in Yellowstone Park, in August, you probably
wouldn't get your feet wet, even wearing sneakers. In most places, the
water barely covers the rocks. This is not a pretty sight for fishermen
and other recreationists. Such low flows can mean that trout will die,
stranded in pools deprived of oxygen, that there will not be enough
water in which to float rafts, and that a picnic along the banks will not
be aesthetically pleasing.

Unfortunately, sights like this one are common on other streams as
well. In 1987 flows in the Ruby River were so low that hundreds of
trout went belly-up in stagnant pools. And just when the fishery was
slowly recovering, another drought in 1994 stressed the fish population. Nearby on the Big Hole, another blue-ribbon trout stream, the
1994 drought increased the demand for irrigation and left flows so low
that fishermen were urged to stay away lest fishing pressure further
stress fish.

The main reason there is so little water at times in these rivers is that
farmers divert most of the flow for irrigation. Under water law in the
West, farmers have secure rights to the water used in agricultural production. Agricultural uses account for approximately 85 percent of
western water withdrawals, leaving urban, industrial, and environmental interests to fight over the remainder. In many cases, the agricultural water is applied to water-intensive crops such as alfalfa, corn,
and sugar beets. The irrigation technology used is typically less than

50 percent efficient, meaning that much of the water diverted for crops runs off fields, carrying with it pesticides, herbicides, and soil nutrients.

Inefficient water use is not confined to agriculture. Urban users who pay low prices for their water plant green lawns in desert cities, let faucets drip continuously, and have antiquated distribution systems that leak badly. Losses from these distribution systems as high as 40 percent are commonplace.

In this setting, water wars often erupt, with environmentalists leading the charge. As David Yardas of the Environmental Defense Fund (EDF) puts it, "Litigation is the norm throughout the West; it has been for a hundred years" (quoted in Lancaster 1990). Environmentalists argue that the water belongs to the people, with the states acting as trustees of the asset. In the case of Mono Lake in California, for example, EDF joined other environmental groups in filing suit in 1983 against the state of California. Using the public trust doctrine, a legal doctrine previously applied mainly to navigation questions, the coalition contended that California had an obligation as trustee of the environment to protect Mono Lake and that it was remiss in allowing Los Angeles to divert so much water that Mono Lake's ecosystem was threatened. The environmental groups wanted Los Angeles to reduce its diversions so that flows into the land-locked sea could be increased. Needless to say, the legal battle was long and acrimonious, but, as we shall see, environmental entrepreneurship played a role in the ultimate resolution of the dispute.

Recreationists seeking public access to streams used similar tactics in Montana. Under the guise of the public trust doctrine, they argued that the water belonged to the citizens of the state and, therefore, private landowners could not deny access for floating and fishing. Fearing that the camel's nose was under the tent and the next step would be to halt irrigation diversions, farmers fought hard. Again, the legal battles were acrimonious. Finally, the legislature waded in with compromise legislation that provided limited public access. Farmers, believing they have legitimate water rights, continue to fear the taking of their lifeblood, while recreationists and environmentalists still argue that instream flows are insufficient to meet their demands. As the sides jostle for legal position, suspicions and fears dominate the winner-takes-all court battles.

Some enviro-capitalists see an alternative approach, one that offers gains for both sides. For them, secure and transferable water rights are the key to balancing traditional consumption with environmental amenities.[1]

Water Brokers

"A Deal That Might Save a Sierra Gem" reads a headline in *Time* (Conniff 1989, 8). "Negotiators are trying to sustain Mono Lake by buying irrigation water from unused fields." The negotiators were none other than officials from EDF, the same organization that participated in the Mono Lake litigation six years earlier. As *Time* said, "the Environmental Defense Fund has a reputation for fighting the new water projects coveted by a lot of farmers." But in this case enviro-capitalist Zach Willey, senior economist for the organization, was acting as a broker between potential buyers and sellers of water. For many years, Willey had been laying the foundation for water marketing ideas with solid research documenting the potential gains from trade among farmers, municipalities, and environmentalists. Once again, he and his partner Tom Graff, an EDF lawyer, were putting their theories to work.

These two were veterans in the water marketing debate. They worked hard to defeat the controversial Peripheral Canal in 1982, a project that would have spent millions of dollars of taxpayers' money to divert water from northern to southern California. Their main argument was that the project did not make economic or environmental sense. As Graff (1982) put it in a *Los Angeles Times* editorial, conservationists believe "that more efficiency [in water allocation] would benefit the environment as well." This led him to ask, "Has all future water-project development been choked off by a new conservationist-conservative alliance . . . ?"

Unfortunately, the alliance has not choked off all water projects that do not pass economic or environmental muster, but Graff and Willey have elevated the status of markets in the water allocation debate. Their work showed that a potential trade between the Imperial Irrigation District and the Municipal Water District was a good deal for both. By lining ditches to prevent leakage, covering ditches to prevent evaporation and monitoring water delivery with computers to ensure efficient use, Willey showed that enough water could be saved to make it worthwhile for the Municipal Water District to pay for improvements in return for the salvaged water.

With the spirit of entrepreneurship and data to support it, Willey and Graff are effective water brokers. With city folks paying more than $250 per acre-foot of water (one foot of water covering one acre or approximately 326,000 gallons) and farmers paying as little as $10 for the same quantity, the potential for win-win trades is enormous. Willey convinces farmers to sell water by pointing out that sales to Los

Angeles can help pay for the labor and water-saving irrigation systems or that revenues from water sales might help pay off the farm's mortgage. But consummating deals is not easy in a world where farmers mistrust environmentalists and fear having their water taken.

It took years, but ultimately Willey and Graff helped finalize a deal that settled the Mono Lake case. When the California State Water Resources Control Board finally ordered Los Angeles to cease diverting water from the Mono Lake watershed, it encouraged water trading as part of the deal, but the sticking point was the cost to Los Angeles. The EDF team's market-based solution suggested that Los Angeles lease irrigation water from farmers in California's Central Valley. They believed that this would be a good source of water because excessive irrigation by those farmers with cheap water from subsidized federal and state projects was causing a buildup of salts and other chemicals in the soil that threatened agricultural productivity and the environment. The EDF proposal called for leasing surplus water from farmers and using the revenues to pay for needed conservation measures. To finance the plan, a 1989 bill pledged state funding of $60 million to protect Mono Lake and compensate Los Angeles for some of its expense in obtaining alternative sources of water. After all, if the environment of Mono Lake was a public value and Los Angeles was relinquishing legitimate water rights, shouldn't the public foot part of the bill? As Graff said, "The idea that the postcard-writing public should pay as well as write cards is not an easy one for preservationists to swallow," but "if there was more of a willingness to pay for maintaining the environment, we wouldn't have to rely on bureaucratic whim" (quoted in Conniff 1989, 8).

Unfortunately, revisions in the legislation governing the Central Valley Project ultimately prevented direct deals with farmers, but their market-based approach was gaining more and more attention. Finally in 1993, a win-win agreement was reached, featuring water transfers from federal and state projects to the city. These transfers were made possible by investments in wastewater reclamation. Flows into Mono Lake have increased in large part due to the brokerage services of the Graff-Willey team.

Willey has now moved to the Pacific Northwest where he is applying his entrepreneurial spirit to the salmon problem. As with water problems that plague California, the endangered status of many salmon and steelhead runs in the Pacific Northwest can be blamed largely on decades of suppressing market forces. Massive federal reclamation projects have subsidized water delivery to farmers, provided low-cost hydroelectric power to industry, and given free recreation to boaters on the many reservoirs along the Columbia River.

With so many subsidized constituents, federal agencies could easily justify building more dams, storing more water, and generating more electricity, all of which have contributed to the demise of Northwest salmon runs. When the dams were built, no one even thought far enough ahead to provide a way for spawning salmon to get upstream. As an afterthought, fish ladders were installed to allow upstream passage, but only recently have biologists realized that downstream migration was perhaps a bigger problem. With the large pools of warmed water behind the dams, salmon smolt have a difficult time avoiding predators and finding their way to the ocean without the aid of current.

Federal proposals to rectify the problems rely on expensive stopgap measures. Agencies are requiring that reservoirs be drawn down to increase stream flows and help guide juvenile salmon on their downstream journey. But smaller pools behind the dams mean less water for irrigation, river transportation, hydroelectric power generation, and recreation. Hence, the salmon may gain (though even this is questionable) but only at the expense of many existing users, who, not surprisingly, are unhappy.

Again, enviro-capitalist Willey has stepped in. Recognizing that incentives matter, Willey has hammered away at legal reforms that allow water marketing to enhance stream flows and has helped to broker a deal to enhance instream flows. From the outset, he recognized that the western water rule of "use it or lose it" was part of the problem, because

> Holders of water rights are often not allowed to resell their rights to others willing to buy them: Idaho's law prohibits sales of diversion rights to out-of-state users—even to protect Idaho salmon. Washington state allows transfers, but only state agencies can hold these rights. Oregon's law discourages water market transactions by skimming portions of any sale into the state's accounts. (Willey 1992)

Willey has championed changes in these state laws to permit the market to help solve the problem.

Working with the Bonneville Power Administration (BPA), the federal power-marketing authority in the Pacific Northwest, Willey helped consummate a deal that will provide between 25,000 and 50,000 acre-feet of additional instream flows, the single largest water transfer from out-of-stream to instream flows in the Northwest. The flows result from a willing buyer-willing seller three-year lease between the BPA and Skyline Farms of Malheur County, Oregon. Skyline Farms, which holds rights to divert water from the Snake and Malheur Rivers, was willing to relinquish its diversion rights in return for payments from electricity producers. Power companies and the BPA will hold the water behind dams for release at times when salmon need it and when it can produce valuable electricity. According to Randy Hardy, BPA administrator,

> The Skyline pilot effort, negotiated between a willing seller and buyer, can demonstrate the energy, environmental, and economic benefits associated with transfers from out-of-stream to instream flows in the Columbia Basin. We're hopeful that the long-term power generation benefits will help us provide more cost-effective fish flow augmentation. To BPA, that makes good economic and environmental sense. The pilot project will also provide an opportunity to work with the local community to mitigate any impact associated with the water transfer.[2]

This water deal lays the groundwork for similar trades throughout the Pacific Northwest. Willey's reports on the Yakima, Snake, and Deschutes River Basins show potential gains from reallocating water diversions to instream flows. Like a broker on the New York Stock Exchange, Willey utilizes a variety of techniques, including standing offers at fixed prices, negotiated leases, water auctions, and option markets. He understands that reforming water use will not be accomplished "by wholesale taking away of resources from industry and farmers, or they're going to wind up litigating you for the next 100 years. You're going to do it through a system of incentives" (quoted in Conniff 1989, 8). In other words, he wants to "buy that fish a drink."

Hay for Fish

While various federal agencies are spending billions of dollars trying to save salmon in the Pacific Northwest, a group of enviro-capitalists is working on a small scale to put its money where its fish are. The Oregon Water Trust was formed in 1993 with the specific mission of restoring surface-water flows in Oregon rivers and streams to protect the fish habitat and other aquatic species on which salmon, steelhead, and other freshwater fish depend for survival. Janet Newman, president of the Oregon Water Trust, believes that the market solutions offer an excellent way to address the problems of declining habitat. As she says,

"In the past there's only been financial incentive for taking water out of streams. We're trying to operate in a noncontentious, cooperative manner that provides incentives for leaving water in streams" (Northwest Area Foundation 1994, 27).

Their first successful effort to provide financial incentives came on Buck Hollow Creek, a tributary of the Deschutes River. Buck Hollow Creek used to teem with spawning steelhead, but spawning runs have dwindled to no more than thirty pairs. The problem is that the stream dries up each year when Rocky Webb, a local rancher, withdraws water to which he has a legal right for irrigation. Webb can remember the healthy population of steelhead from his days growing up on the ranch, and he wants to see the steelhead thrive again in Buck Hollow Creek. But, as he points out, "I also have a bottom line to worry about" (quoted in Laatz 1994).

Andrew Purkey of the Oregon Water Trust saw a chance to help the steelhead by helping Rocky Webb's bottom line. He negotiated a deal with the rancher whereby Webb agreed to stop irrigating fifty acres of hay ground in return for $6,600, the profit he earned from seventy-eight tons of hay produced on the field in 1993. Funds for the deal came from a three-year, $370,000 grant from the Northwest Area Foundation of St. Paul, Minnesota. The trust hopes that these flows, combined with efforts to restore streamside vegetation and to fence cattle away from the banks, will increase to 500 pairs the number of steelhead returning to the creek.

Webb is happy with the outcome that benefits both sides. "I see it as a step for the positive to make people realize there are workable solutions out there. . . . I think anytime you have an agreement between a rancher or agriculture and an organization, it's good. It opens itself up to more possibilities" (quoted in Laatz 1994). Aided by the Oregon Water Trust, Webb is able to make water from hay rather than the other way around.

One More for the Road

Reversing the "morning after" effects of the Newlands Project in western Nevada called for entrepreneurial skill of the highest order. This federal irrigation project, named for the key sponsor of the Reclamation Act of 1902, dammed and diverted for irrigation the Truckee and Carson Rivers into the arid, sage-covered Lahontan Valley. As the diversions made that desert "bloom like a rose," the wetlands around the Stillwater National Wildlife Refuge sixty miles east of Reno, began to dry up. Once covering 100,000 acres, the wetlands shrank to 7,000 acres and became polluted with trace elements leached from the soil and with pesticides, herbicides, and fertilizer carried in the agricultural runoff. Once a haven for millions of waterfowl and fish, the wetlands became an ecological disaster when 7 million fish died in 1987, and waterfowl populations plummeted to 40 percent of the normal levels.

Enviro-capitalists from EDF and the Nature Conservancy then stepped in. For decades, environmentalists knew there was problem at Stillwater and searched in despair for a solution that would return the marsh's lifeblood. Though EDF's David Yardas recognizes that litigation is the norm in such disputes, he understands that win-win solutions hold more promise for Stillwater. As he notes, "What we're trying to do is bring . . . economic considerations into the water-use calculus" (quoted in Lancaster 1990).

David Livermore, director of the conservancy's Great Basin field office in Salt Lake City, began the brokering process. Because the conservancy is famous for using markets to save sensitive environmental lands, Ron Anglin, manager of the Stillwater National Wildlife Refuge, turned to that organization. "The Nature Conservancy was the best group to get involved and work with the issues. They were able to get in there and . . . work through some of the legal problems that we couldn't work through" (quoted in Vetter 1991, 24). "This was not a case where we could have gone out and bought 40 acres in the middle of Stillwater in an effort to save the marsh. That would have been like sticking our heads in the sand," said Livermore, when he began working on the project (quoted in Vetter 1991, 24). This project was not typical for the conservancy because it involved water rather than land. Moreover, it was complicated by multiple parties, including farmers, communities built around agriculture, federal bureaucracies, an Indian tribe, and environmentalists.

Livermore and his colleagues rolled up their sleeves and went to work. As he put it, "We had to take traditional real estate skills that we have developed over the years and adapt them to the water marketplace. It basically came down to our adapting water marketing techniques for wildlife preservation" (quoted in Vetter 1991, 26). The Nature Conservancy became the primary broker between farmers with water rights and federal and state agencies. Initially, it relied on purchases of agricultural lands and their accompanying water rights with the objective of retiring the lands from agricultural production and returning the water to the Stillwater marsh.

The conservancy set a goal of purchasing 20,000 acre-feet of water by 1993, far from the 55,000 acre-feet biologists believe is necessary to support 25,000 acres of wetlands. Undaunted by U.S. Fish and Wildlife Service (FWS) estimates that meeting the more ambitious goal would cost $50 million, the conservancy began by providing $1.5 million in private funds to purchase land and water rights. The first purchase came from Fallon, Nevada, farmer Mike Casey, who received more than $135,000 for water rights used on his 150 acres of farmland. According to Graham Chisholm, the conservancy's field officer in Nevada who took over responsibility for brokering water transfers, 14,000 acre-feet had been purchased by 1994.

To leverage its $1.5 million, the conservancy has teamed up with the state of Nevada, which has provided another $2.5 million. Though the conservancy-state team has far less money than the FWS, which has $10 to $12 million for purchasing water rights, the conservancy and the state have been far more effective. Both efforts generally purchase land and water with the intention of retiring the land from agricultural production and returning the water to Stillwater. The big difference is that the conservancy and the state do not retain the land while the FWS does. By reselling the land, the conservancy and the state can reinvest their funds in more water and get a much bigger "bang-for-the-buck." Though their combined expenditures have been 70 percent less than those of the FWS, the conservancy-state water purchases have accounted for nearly 60 percent of the total.

Even though water trading was between willing buyers and willing sellers, the community was nevertheless concerned about an end to the agricultural way of life. Hence, farmers were not always eager to negotiate. As Ted deBraga, a rancher who sold 1,200 acre-feet of water for $360,000 and retired 500 acres from farming, said, "It's surprising how many [neighbors] have come to me and told me they would sell their [water rights] but they won't tell their neighbors" (quoted in Lancaster 1990).

Recognizing that the agricultural community of Churchill County would be skeptical of environmentalists, the conservancy has done much more than raise money and broker water trades. It worked with the Soil Conservation Service to convene a local working group to develop a rating system to rank potential acquisitions. The Land Evaluation and Siting Assessment (LESA) system incorporates community criteria, including local planning objectives, aquifer recharge, and agricultural productivity. Using this rating system to identify lands and water to be purchased has helped diffuse potential opposition. The conservancy has also implemented innovative acquisition strategies that include various forms of leasing and options for "interruptible sources." It has also devised an auction system whereby interested willing sellers submit bids ranked on a combined basis of the LESA rating and the price. The conservancy has developed a land exchange program that allows owners to exchange private land for public land with the stipulation that the water rights associated with the private land be returned to Stillwater, and the public land not be developed. A local land bank also has been established. A landowner who wants to sell productive agricultural land can put his land and water into the bank. The productive land can be brought back into production by retiring marginal farm land and transferring the water from it to the more productive land in the bank. Graham Chisholm is also exploring the possibility of establishing a water bank in Lahontan Reservoir. This bank would allow water owners to save water in the Bureau of Reclamation reservoir for later use or for sale to others. Chisholm thinks that this might provide a way of purchasing water in wetter years when it is cheaper and saving it for drier years when it is more valuable to the Stillwater ecosystem. As Chisholm says, "You need a real diverse tool box, and it won't work without that."[3] This is what enviro-capitalism is all about.

Trumpeting Water Markets

The drought of 1987–88 that caused the wildfires in Yellowstone Park also made fishermen and environmentalists keenly aware of the importance of instream flows. But even before the streams were drying up that summer, problems were manifesting themselves in the winter on the Henry's Fork of the Snake River in Idaho, home to nearly one-fourth of North America's magnificent trumpeter swans. As many westerners put up with the inconvenience of stalled cars, frozen pipes, and closed schools, the trumpeter swans struggled for survival. Normally, the Henry's Fork does not freeze because it is fed by constant-temperature spring waters. Severe cold and below-normal stream flows, however, caused the river to freeze solidly, cutting the birds off from the aquatic plants on which they feed. At least fifty swans died.

Fortunately, releases from upstream reservoirs belonging to irrigators increased the flows sufficiently to raise water temperatures and clear a free-flowing channel before more swans died. How did biologists get the irrigators to release the water on which they depend for summer crops? They used enviro-capitalism.

Initially, the Snake River Water District donated 1,600 acre-feet to increase flows, but when this proved insufficient, Ruth Shee of the Trumpeter Swan Society and Guy Bonnivier of the Nature Conservancy began negotiating for even more water. On 1 February 1989, the conservancy immediately loaned $8,000 to purchase 3,200 acre-feet of water from the Upper Snake Water Bank. This loan was later repaid by the U.S. Fish and Wildlife Service ($4,000), the Idaho Department of Fish and Game ($1,000), and individual donors, including a donation from the city of Grand Prairie, Alberta (Canada). On 3 February, the Trumpeter Swan Society added another 3,200 acre-feet by committing another $8,000, and irrigators donated another 10,000 acre-feet to the cause. The deal struck between the enviro-capitalist representatives of the swans and the farmers provided that farmers would maintain flows at 400 cubic-feet-per-second (up from 100) to break the ice jam. In return, the farmers would receive compensation for the released water *if* reservoir levels did not replenish themselves. This contingency contract proved successful for both sides. Some of the released water was replenished, making the arrangement less expensive than initially anticipated for the Nature Conservancy and the Trumpeter Swan Society.

To avoid a recurrence of the problem, the two groups have negotiated a long-term contract that guarantees a flow of 200 cubic feet per second, the amount deemed necessary to prevent freeze-up. This contingent flow comes from Idaho's water bank. Like other water banks throughout the West, Idaho's bank allows water owners, mainly farmers, to deposit excess water and receive compensation if the water is purchased by others. Hence, farmers with innovative ways of reducing their water needs can profit when enviro-capitalists want to purchase that water for instream flows.

Dollars Run Through It

Robert Redford's film *A River Runs Through It*, based on Norman Maclean's story of fly-fishing and family loyalty, sparked the interest of thousands of would-be fly casters who flocked to their local tackle shops and mail-order catalogues. Then they purchased their plane tickets, flew to Montana, rented cars, and headed for the nearest stream with public access. When they got to the streams, bedecked in their

$200 waders and carrying their $500 fly rods, however, they found the wide-open spaces filmed by Redford filled with other fly-fishing aficionados flailing the water for weary trout. Instead of providing pristine, untried waters, the public access sites are often littered, overcrowded, and overfished. Even when the angler tries to escape by floating the legendary Yellowstone, Madison, or Big Hole, he still finds the river nearly bank to bank with boats.

The enviro-capitalists found niches here for providing private access to uncrowded streams managed for fishing. Even before Redford began reaping profits from fly-fishing, Edwin Nelson of Pray, Montana, was profiting from his own fishing asset. Located in the Paradise Valley just north of Yellowstone Park, Nelson's Spring Creek offers some of the finest fishing in the United States. The creek is fed by a constant flow of spring water that maintains a temperature ideal for rainbow, brown, and cutthroat trout. For his part, Nelson has done little more than leave the stream alone. Cattle are kept back from the banks so that vital cover is not destroyed and withdrawals for irrigation are minimized. Because the spring originates on private property, no one else can tap it for irrigation and threaten instream flows for trout. Nelson receives $50 per day for each of six rods allowed during the spring, summer, and fall periods. There are no crowds, the scenery is spectacular, and the fishing is superb. From June through September, the stream is fully booked so the fish have lots of experience recognizing imitation flies presented by hopeful anglers. Some days, hundreds of fish boil on the surface in response to a fly hatch, but it still takes skill to hook and land one.

Nelson's success prompted two other landowners in the area to capitalize on their spring creeks. Both Armstrong's and Depuy's Spring Creeks offer similar fishing experiences at competitive prices, allowing ten to fifteen rods per day. In the Depuy case, the potential profits from fee fishing made it possible for the owner Eva Depuy to hire a "stream doctor" to restore bank vegetation, refill gravel beds, and reconstruct riffles, thus returning the creek to its natural state.

In California, where the population is denser than in Montana, fee fisheries in the northern part of the state offer catch-and-release, fly-fishing-only experiences comparable to those in Montana. One of the best private fishing programs is run by Mike Michalak's Fly Shop in Redding. The shop has leases with seven ranchers ranging from five to ten years in duration. A lease on the Hat Creek Ranch near Mt. Lassen National Park, an hour and twenty minutes from Redding, allows access to Hat Creek, an improved meadow stream, as well as to two lakes. Fish from the stream average fourteen to sixteen inches in length, with a few reaching twenty-four inches. Abundant insect hatches make the fish prolific but challenging. Hat Creek Ranch offers accommodations, meals, and fishing for $175 per person per day. Similar opportunities can be had at Coffee Cup Lake, Clear Creek, Goodrich Creek, Riverside, and Rainbow Lake, and others.

The strategy of the Fly Shop is to contract with ranchers where streams are degraded due to grazing and to invest in reclamation. All of the leases have one common denominator: because the fish and their habitat are an asset, the owners manage them to maximize the experience for the paying customer. When Mike Michalak started leasing, he had to convince ranchers that this was a good idea by offering them cash for fishing rights, provided the stream was upgraded. Now, ranchers contact Mike to see if their property has potential for fishing. Instead of a race to streams crowded with other fishermen, supplies are racing to meet the market demand.

Though fee fishing in the United States is still new, the system has long been the norm on trout streams and salmon rivers in Great Britain. There, fishing rights have been privately owned for centuries. Those unfamiliar with the British system may think that it means only the wealthy nobility can enjoy a day of angling, but, as with restaurants or shopping malls, the marketplace for fishing in England offers a full range of options. Some of the best fishing beats are owned by the wealthy, while others are owned by small villages, pubs, and fishing clubs. To ensure that conditions are pleasurable for anglers, the rivers are divided into "beats" about two kilometers long usually with no more than three rods on each beat at a given time. At one extreme, the Houghton Fishing Club has only twenty upper-crust members and often hosts the Prince of Wales. The value of Houghton's fishing rights is said to be worth around $30 million.[4] But the untitled can easily become members of a syndicated trout fishing outlet with a price of $750 per year, entitling the member to fish one day per week. The Greyhound Inn, a bed and breakfast in Stockbridge, owns a few hundred yards on the Test River running directly behind the inn. The owner Andy McCall allows two fishermen at a time to fish the beat for $45 per person per day. Looking to expand its market in England, the Orvis Company, a famous American fly-fishing and outdoor equipment company, purchased fishing rights to beats on England's Test and Itchen. Orvis offers highly affordable day fishing and angling classes to aspiring English fly-fishers for about $180. The cost includes a "gillie" to outfit and guide you to where fish lie in wait for your fly.

Not only do the private fishing rights in England provide access to excellent fishing, they provide the incentive to ensure quality, uncrowded fishing experiences. Fishing on the Allen, the Test, and the Itchen commands a higher price because they are better managed. Cattle are fenced away from the banks, weeds are controlled, and, perhaps most importantly, the number of fishermen is limited. An avid American fisherman, Clifford Russell, described his experience on the Allen River as "beautiful, productive, and challenging fishing" with "no worries about who—and how many—may be around the next bend. No fear that you are fishing over a pool emptied by the careless wading and casting of some competitor. Better one week per year of bliss than every weekend on one of Pennsylvania's crowded limestone streams" (quoted in Shaw and Stroup 1988, 34).

Similarly, in northern Scotland, famous salmon rivers such as the Brora, the Cassley, the Carron, the Helmsdale, the Naver, and the Oykel are in high demand because quality is assured through private fishing rights. While most of the great salmon rivers in the United States have been adversely affected by hydroelectric dams, the Scottish rivers remain relatively untouched. The rights to fish these rivers are held by individuals or syndicates, and anyone wishing to wet a fly there can arrange it through one of the small local hotels that own fishing rights or rent a private lodge through estate managers who specialize in fishing leases. Fishing on one of these rivers costs about $1,500 per rod per day. Two or three anglers can split the cost and alternate fishing.

Because British fishing rights are so valuable, enviro-capitalists who own them have the economic incentive to protect their investments from polluters. Owners of fishing rights act as unpaid policemen, monitoring England's inland waters for pollution. Using the common law, the Anglers' Co-operative Association (ACA, recently renamed the Anglers' Conservation Association) has represented owners in court cases where they must prove that pollution is damaging fishing and causing economic harm.

The ACA, brainchild of entrepreneur and fly-fisherman John Eastwood, was formed in 1948 to lower the costs of coordinating the actions of the many owners, each of whom might be damaged slightly by pollution, and to provide the technical expertise necessary to pursue legal actions. ACA members include individuals, fishing clubs, country inns, and communities who own or lease fishing rights and pay an annual membership fee. In return, the association "indemnifies them against the legal costs of bringing action under common law" (Bate 1994, 14). "The association won its first major pollution case in

1951 against two chemical companies and the city of Derby for pumping untreated sewage, hot water, and tar products into the River Derwent" (Shaw and Stroup 1988, 36). Since then, the ACA has been successful in obtaining both injunctions to stop pollution and clean up rivers and damages to compensate owners for losses. From 1985 to 1992, the ACA won more than $1,125,000 in damages. By the end of 1994, the ACA represented more than 17,500 members and had brought over 2,000 actions against polluters. Remarkably, the association has lost only two cases (Bate 1994, 14).

On streams famous for their salmon fishing, conflicts can arise between those with netting rights at the mouth of the river and sportfishers with upstream angling rights. Given the secure rights, however, these conflicts can be and have been resolved by purchasing netting rights. The Atlantic Salmon Conservation Trust is a nonprofit group that has purchased 280 netting rights at a cost of $2.1 million and expects to reduce the netting catch of salmon by 25 percent. Salar Properties takes another approach. It purchases ocean netting rights and resells them on a time-share basis to recreational fishermen. Envirocapitalist Andrew C. Coombs from Salar Properties says his company takes action "where we see an opportunity to substantially improve the management effort, and consequently hopefully improve the fishing and its value" (quoted in Shaw and Stroup 1988, 37). Making a profit in the process is what enviro-capitalism is all about.

Call the Doctor

When Ted Turner bought the 21,000-acre Bar-None Ranch and the 107,000-acre Flying D Ranch, he not only wanted to give bison a home on the range, he wanted to see wild trout dancing at the end of his flyline. The only problem was that the two streams running through his property had few fish because they had been trashed by years of cattle grazing the banks. But this did not deter Turner, who hired Inter-Fluve, Inc., the same company that turned an irrigation ditch into a spawning channel for the Boise River brown trout and created several hundred feet of new trout stream for Peter O'Neill's River Run housing development (see chapter 1). After surveying Sixteen Mile Creek and Cherry Creek, an Inter-Fluve hydrologist, Dale Miller, concluded that "the habitat was limited." Stream banks were in poor condition with few hiding and spawning areas for trout. Inter-Fluve stabilized streambanks with a concoction made from coconut skins, planted cover vegetation, and created meanders with gravel for spawning. Trout numbers have risen dramatically from these changes, and the stream doctors, as they are known, made a handsome profit.

The entrepreneurs behind Inter-Fluve are Dale Miller, Bob O'Brien, and Greg Koonce. In 1983, they began Timberland Reclamations but later changed the name to Inter-Fluve to reflect the company's pioneering approach to stream reclamation. Interfluve means a joining of several streams into one; the company's approach was to blend a variety of disciplines into one. Hence, the staff includes experts in hydrology, geomorphology, fisheries biology, landscape architecture, and geology. Says Miller, "We rely heavily on natural materials to get the natural healing process going." For example, they lay coconut fiber mats on stream banks to hold them in place; they use log structures to deflect currents; and they plant native vegetation to provide cover for the trout. But Inter-Fluve is also not afraid to use a heavier hand when necessary; hence, its tools include bulldozers, earthmovers, and dump trucks. When they are finished using these techniques, the patient is healthier.

Inter-Fluve can convert an unsightly irrigation ditch into a fertile trout stream, complete with spawning channels, bring a river back to life after it has been polluted by mine tailings, create a spring creek with water pumped from deep wells and recirculating pumps, or build a Walden Pond from the bottom up. The company has even built a trout stream for the government of the United Arab Emirates on a man-made "leisure island" in the Persian Gulf. Prices for a house call from the stream doctors range from $5 to $20 per foot of stream reclaimed.

"The stream amenity is an ever-increasing market," says Bob O'Brien, one of the cofounders. In 1995, Inter-Fluve topped $2 million in sales and employed twenty doing business with Ted Turner, Atlantic Richfield, Dupont, and Burlington Northern. Business is going so well that the company spends less than 1 percent of gross sales on advertising, relying instead on references and reputation. From its two offices in Bozeman, Montana, and Hood River, Oregon, Inter-Fluve manages projects in the United States, Argentina, Mexico, Scotland, and New Zealand.

Inter-Fluve is successful because landowners want and can afford to take better care of their trout streams. In cases such as the Flying D Ranch, the goal was to improve fishing for the owners and their friends. But in other cases, it is the rising demand for high-quality fishing that is driving the reclamation market. Ranchers are beginning to recognize that their creeks are another asset, as long as they can restrict access, charge fees, and provide a high-quality fishing experience.

Going with the Flow

The possibilities seem endless for enviro-capitalists to improve the water environment in the United States. From water trades to fee fishing to stream rehabilitation, profit and not-for-profit entrepreneurs alike are discovering that it pays to go with the flow of rising recreational and environmental demands for water. From an institutional standpoint, the last fifteen years have seen a growing shift away from costly command-and-control approaches to water allocation that have locked most of the West's water into agricultural uses. Environmental Defense Fund economist and water broker Zach Willey understands that shifting water to environmental uses requires a market approach: "You're not going do it by wholesale taking away of resources from industry and farmers. . . . You're going to do it through a system of incentives." As an enviro-capitalist, Willey's approach is to "go out and make some deals" (quoted in Conniff 1989).

Making those deals should be relatively easy under the western prior appropriation system that clearly defines rights to water. Entrepreneurs like Zach Willey and Andrew Purkey can go to state agencies and discover who owns water and hence with whom they must deal.

States can also impede these deals because laws often prohibit willing buyer-willing seller trades. Because most states do not consider private ownership of instream flows a beneficial use, water rights transferred from legitimate agricultural uses to instream uses can be forfeited. Often it is only state or federal agencies that can claim water for instream uses.

Montana is typical. Until 1988 there was almost no way that diversion rights could be retired to be left instream. That year, however, the legislature passed legislation allowing the Department of Fish, Wildlife, and Parks to bargain with farmers on a very limited basis to return water to streams for fish and wildlife purposes. Even this minor step toward water marketing was opposed by farmers who feared that environmental and recreational interests would get enough money to buy up all agricultural water. When this did not happen and when farmers realized that making deals could reallocate water without acrimony, their resistance to water marketing softened. Today, Montana law allows environmental and recreational interests to lease agricultural water, though still on a limited basis.

Such changes indicate the growing pressure to follow Willey's strategy. Several states are recognizing the growing demand for instream flows and seeking ways to make this happen without taking water from status quo users. Making deals requires well-defined *and* transferable water rights. Without the latter, enviro-capitalists cannot act on their entrepreneurial insights. With transferability between willing environmental buyers and willing agricultural sellers, Mark Twain's adage that "Whiskey is for drinkin' and water is for fightin'" can be laid to rest.

Notes

1. For a general discussion of water marketing, see Anderson and Snyder (1997).

2. Quoted in EDF press release, 13 July 1994, "EDF, Federal Energy Agency Announce Water Project."

3. Telephone interview with Graham Chisholm, 17 February 1995.

4. Conversions from pounds were made assuming £1 is equivalent to approximately $1.50 in U.S. dollars.

References

Anderson, Terry L., and Pamela S. Snyder. 1997. *In Search of Water Markets: Priming the Invisible Pump*. Washington, DC: Cato Institute.

Bate, Roger. 1994. Water Pollution Prevention: A Nuisance Approach. *Economic Affairs* 14(3): 13–14.

Conniff, Richard. 1989. A Deal That Might Save a Sierra Gem. *Time*, April 3.

Graff, Thomas J. 1982. Future Water Plans Need a Trickle-Up Economizing. *Los Angeles Times*, June 13.

Laatz, Joan. 1994. Rancher Leases Water Rights to Keep Stream Full for Salmon. *Oregonian*, June 19.

Lancaster, John. 1990. Buying Peace in Western Water War. *Washington Post*, June 10.

Northwest Area Foundation. 1994. *Annual Report*. St. Paul, MN: Northwest Area Foundation.

Shaw, Jane S., and Richard L. Stroup. 1988. Gone Fishin': Britain's Streams Are Lovely, Clear, and Deep. *Reason*, August/September.

Vetter, Don. 1991. Teeming Oasis or Desert Mirage? *Nature Conservancy*, September/October.

Willey, Zach. 1992. Freer Markets Would Protect Northwest Salmon. *Wall Street Journal*, March 9.

Chapter 6

Eco-Developers

There are some who can live without wild things, and some who cannot.

—Aldo Leopold, Foreword to *A Sand County Almanac*

Dayton Hyde, former eastern Oregon rancher and current guardian of feral horses in South Dakota, combines a unquenchable thirst for nature with a fiery entrepreneurial spirit. He believes that one can profit from the earth while profiting it as well. On his 6,000-acre Yamsi Ranch in Klamath County, Oregon, Hyde turned 2,000 acres of what he called "scrubby worthless grazing land and lodgepole forest" into habitat rich in fish and wildlife.[1] His main efforts included creating a sixty-foot deep lake with a three-and-one-half-mile shoreline, replete with rainbow trout weighing up to fourteen pounds, thousands of migrating ducks and geese, endangered bald eagles, ospreys, sandhill cranes, loons, and trumpeter swans. Hyde also restored wetlands in 25 percent of his pasturelands, previously drained to create hay fields.

According to Hyde, the combination of wetlands and lake improved the productivity of his ranch in a number of ways. It provided warmer irrigation water that moderated the local climate, thereby reducing the incidence of frost damage to crops. It attracted more song birds that helped control grasshopper damage. It improved the productivity of his pastureland so that beef production doubled on the acres devoted to grazing.

Committed to his cause, Hyde has written several books on wildlife and its relationship to ranching, lectured on his approach to other ranchers, and founded Operation Stronghold, a nonprofit foundation dedicated to promoting wildlife habitat on private lands across the United States (Hyde 1986). Through the work of his foundation, Hyde has discovered that many ranchers will devise innovative ways to enhance the natural amenities on their land, just as he has done on his, *if* they are given half a chance.

Why the big if? The rest of Hyde's story explains this. He invested in wildlife projects amounting to $200,000 partly because he was committed to enhancing the land's natural amenities, partly because he could increase the land's productivity, and partly because he figured that the amenity values would increase the marketability of his land should he want to sell it. In fact, he entertained the idea of eventually subdividing part of his land and selling smaller parcels to people seeking retirement or second homes—people who enjoyed wildlife and were willing to live by Hyde's rules. By carefully selecting areas to minimize disturbance to wildlife and by placing protective covenants on the land, Hyde felt that he could capitalize on what he had created and still protect it.

Hyde tried to implement his plan a few years later, but by that time any hope of developing the land and recouping part of the wildlife investments had been wiped out. In 1973, Oregon adopted a new land use law that prevented the conversion of "prime" agricultural land to other uses. Lawyers advised Hyde that the rules were so strict that it would be foolhardy even to try subdividing. He considered selling to a developer who might fight the zoning battle but decided not to because the court costs and legal fees would substantially reduce the amount he would net on the land.

To make matters worse, Hyde's extraordinary accomplishments created another ill-timed liability. In Hyde's words, "federal regulators had the authority to shut me down anytime, without compensating me." In addition to creating wetlands that were subject to federal regulation, Hyde was providing habitat for endangered bald eagles as well as a rare species of algae that grows only in six isolated places in the world. He knew that if regulators found out about these rare species on his ranch they could use the Endangered Species Act to control his land use and hence his property value. Hyde notes, "Ranchers don't have a lot to play with when it comes to making a profit. Take some of their assets or prevent them from using some of their assets, and they can easily go broke." Ironically, though Hyde wanted to show federal biologists what could be done to produce more wildlife on a working cattle ranch, he must have had concerns about possible regulations.

Would Dayton Hyde have chosen to make the habitat improvements if he had anticipated these regulatory constraints? The answer is probably yes, because he is committed to good stewardship and because the investments did increase other productivity on his ranch. Today,

Hyde's family still operates Yamsi Ranch in the same nurturing manner. Hyde himself has taken on a new cause in South Dakota where he operates an 11,000-acre ranch that provides a private sanctuary for wild horses orphaned from federal lands. His new operation is nonprofit, and he supports it with donations, fee-based nature tours, and anything "he can think of to keep afloat." He also has organized Operation Stronghold, a loosely knit group of private landowners dedicated to good resource stewardship.

According to Hyde, the organization brings both good news and bad news. The good news is that most landowners are more than willing to do more for wildlife. The bad news is that under the current regulatory environment many are afraid to try, fearing the wrath of regulators. In other words, for anyone enhancing the natural environment with the expectation of later marketing the improvements, the government's message is let the seller beware.

The constraints on Dayton Hyde have not thwarted all eco-developers. As we saw in chapter 1, Peter O'Neill has done well by melding his subdivisions with stream reclamation. Other success stories tell how landowners have used innovative contracts to preserve and capitalize on environmental amenities. Moreover, open space and wildlife habitat can be preserved through "private regulations" in the form of protective covenants, a tool used increasingly by entrepreneurs in the land trust movement.

Hilton Head's Heros

The *Fifteenth Annual Report of the Council on Environmental Quality* called Hilton Head one of "the most sensitively developed vacation and recreational complexes in the country" (Smith 1984, 402). Hilton Head Island lies off the coast of South Carolina, thirty miles north of Savannah, Georgia, and ninety miles south of Charleston, South Carolina. Approximately forty-two square miles in area, it is one of the largest coastal barrier islands between New Jersey and Florida. Natural amenities abound on this subtropical island. The interior is heavily forested with a wide variety of trees and shrubs, including live and water oaks, black gums, bay trees, and southern magnolias. The sound side has salt marshes and a network of creeks, lagoons, and wetlands. Wildlife is abundant and includes 260 species of birds, alligators, bobcats, white-tailed deer, raccoons, and wild turkeys.

Hilton Head has a rich history. It was discovered by the Spanish in

1526 and named for the English Captain William Hilton in 1663. Beginning in the 1700s, the English employed a plantation system of agriculture, raising indigo, rice, and cotton through the 1850s. During the Civil War, the Union used it as a military base, when it already had two newspapers, hotels, a theater, and a hospital. Following the Civil War, Hilton Head reverted to its agricultural traditions until 1956 when a bridge to the island was completed.

In the early 1950s, Charles E. Fraser was the developer who pioneered environmentally sensitive development on the Hilton Head, beginning with Sea Pines Plantation. As owner of 40 percent of the island, Fraser's vision was to set aside nature preserves alongside carefully planned development that would maintain property values for island residents. His approach was all the more amazing because it occurred before the 1970s rise of environmental consciousness.

Fraser understood the importance of legal contracts in preserving the natural and resort environment. He used protective covenants to safeguard his contributions to the island's private nature preserve system and other natural areas within development complexes. His strict property association by-laws included private regulations of the number, location, and size of billboards and directional signs, predating the national highway beautification laws and local sign codes.

The initial covenant for Sea Pines permanently set aside 1,280 acres of woodlands and open spaces, one-fourth of the resort's total land area. This included the 605-acre Sea Pines Forest Preserve that is leased to the state of South Carolina as a wildlife sanctuary but maintained by the Sea Pines property owners' association. The preserve has important stands of climax forest, two major trail systems, a security force, and a full-time wildlife officer.

Sea Pines has other smaller areas protected as well. For example, the fifty-acre Pocosin Preserve, created in 1963, contains native vegetation characteristic of the Carolina coastal lowlands. At the request of island resident Caroline Newhall, Charles Fraser donated the area to the Hilton Head Audubon Society to preserve "the native vegetation of Hilton Head Island in an easily accessible area for all to enjoy" (Smith 1984, 405).

Sea Pines and the other resort plantations on the island also have protected archaeological and historical sites. Located within Sea Pines Forest Preserve is an Indian shell ring consisting of a circular mound of oyster shells, animal bones, and pottery fragments that dates back to 1450 B.C. Next to the preserve is Heritage Farm, where old plantation crops of sea island cotton, indigo, sugar cane, tobacco, and rice are still cultivated and where windmill pumps and mule-powered sugar mills produce cane syrup.

Hilton Head Plantation was developed in ways that protect the environment and preserve the island's heritage. Like the other island developments, Hilton Head Plantation has a master plan and an architectural board that oversees building codes and tree preservation. This board must approve development plans for individual lots and grant permission to fell trees over six inches in diameter. In addition, more than 250,000 trees—mainly southern pine—have been planted, and reforestation is scheduled for land that was logged before the development. Where the popular golf courses were built, care was taken to protect wildlife habitat and to design a lagoon system with proper drainage for protecting salt marshes and oyster beds.

One of the refuges on Hilton Head Plantation is the 137-acre Whooping Crane Pond Conservancy, owned and managed by the property owners' association of Hilton Head Conservancy. The refuge protects forests, wetlands, flora, and fauna and provides an important rookery for about 250 pairs of colonial nesting herons, egrets, and ibises. A 1,500-foot trail and 1,086-foot boardwalk wind through pine forest, boggy bottom land, swamp, and sawgrass savanna habitats. Another important refuge is the fifty-acre Cypress Conservancy that contains a pond cypress swamp with a small egret rookery.

The other resort plantations also have their share of protected areas. The Port Royal Plantation, for example, has a six-acre arboretum with a significant collection of 100 native plants. It also has the fourteen-acre Sherman Preserve, protecting a historical site of Civil War breastworks and a beautiful forested area. A small rookery is located in the Spanish Wells Plantation.

Rapidly accelerating land values and continued growth in the 1980s brought added pressures to this island paradise. Local environmentalists contend that developers have built too close to the marshes, causing pollution from nonpoint runoff. They believe that recent developers have shown less appreciation for wildlife habitat and water resources on Hilton Head. Ed Drane of the Hilton Head Sierra Club laments the fact that years ago, when land values were much lower, it was far easier to set aside large amounts of land as open space or nature preserves.

Though continued development undoubtedly is putting pressure on the island's environment, it is important to recall what made Hilton Head so desirable in the first place: It was Charles Fraser's private, profitable vision for a environmentally sensitive development. Even critics of growth on Hilton Head Island such as Ed Drane recognize the early achievements of this innovative developer. His concept was risky, but he rose to the challenge. Recent concerns do not negate the value of his original approach but raise new challenges for future eco-developers.

Big Sky's Bounty

Just before Earth Day on 22 April 1970, ground was broken on a major ski and summer resort forty-five miles from the northern border of Yellowstone Park. A dream of the late Chet Huntley, television news anchorman in the 1960s, Big Sky of Montana was supposed to bring jobs to his native state while protecting the environment he loved so much. The resort is located in a high mountain valley that drains into the Gallatin River, a blue-ribbon trout stream where Huntley loved to fish. The ski slopes are located high on Lone Mountain, a spectacular conical peak surrounded by the Lee Metcalf Wilderness Area. Land within and around the resort provides winter habitat for Yellowstone Park's large elk herd and for bighorn sheep from the nearby Spanish Peaks. Grizzly bears are sometimes spotted in meadows not far from the golf course.

During the planning stage, designers of the project imagined a large residential-resort community that would capitalize on the area's amenities. A consortium of major corporations, including Chrysler Realty, Northwest Airlines, and Burlington Northern Railroad, purchased private land homesteaded in the late 1800s or granted to the railroad as part of its land grant. Then it traded sections of railroad land grants in other parts of the Gallatin National Forest for federal land within the consortium's planned development. This trading provided the consortium with 8,000 acres of private land on which it could control development and also consolidated land holdings elsewhere for the U.S. Forest Service, making its management easier.

Fledgling environmental groups opposed the development on the grounds that it was being built in a pristine ecosystem sandwiched between a national park and a wilderness area. They were concerned about air and water quality, wildlife habitat, scenery, and congestion. It is reasonable to assume that, had these environmental groups had the clout of their counterparts who ten years later stopped a similar resort closer to Yellowstone's boundary, they would have stopped Big Sky, too.

Interestingly, the same concerns that motivated environmental groups drove the development corporation to consolidate private lands. Because they planned to profit from the amenities, the corporation wanted to avoid what Huntley once referred to as "the corrugated iron bar-and-beanery with neon signs." Hence, before subdividing the land and selling parcels for homes, condominiums, and businesses, the corporation added strict legal covenants to the deeds. The covenants allowed it to capitalize on the amenities by ensuring that future development at Big Sky would blend with the area's natural surroundings long after the property had been transferred to others. Because potential buyers knew that all other landowners had to adhere to rules protecting the area's natural surroundings, they were willing to pay a premium for the land. Even though ownership of the resort has changed hands since Huntley's initial dream began to take shape, development has continued, more people frequent the area, wildlife numbers continue to increase, air and water quality has not deteriorated, and property values have risen. All of this occurred because the original developers understood how to protect and market Big Sky's environment. Certainly Chet Huntley cared about the environment of his native state, but it was more than concern that motivated the well-financed consortium. Those entrepreneurs recognized the growing demand for amenities and profited by preserving them.

The protection and development at Big Sky has created positive spillovers for nearby property owners. Certainly, the initial corporation would have liked to capture all of these positive spillovers by owning more property, but both capital and vision always have limits. As the market has unfolded, however, other entrepreneurs are filling a niche.

The most recent example of enviro-capitalism is the development of Moonlight Basin Ranch, a 25,000-acre project located between Big Sky and Ennis, Montana. Lee Poole, one of the three owners, describes Moonlight Basin as "a privatized version of a national park" (quoted in Ellig 1995). Judging from its natural features, he may not be too far off.

Moonlight Basin Ranch encompasses most of the Jack Creek drainage in the Gallatin Range. The landscape includes rugged mountains, alpine forests, lush meadows, and snow-fed streams. The private land in Jack Creek is surrounded by the rugged, roadless Lee Metcalf Wilderness Area where elk, grizzly bears, mountain goats, mountain sheep, and moose roam, and maybe some day wolves will howl.

In July 1992, Poole and his partners, fellow Ennis resident Joe Vujovich and Ohio businessman Keith Brown, purchased the property from Plum Creek Timber Company, which inherited it from the original Northern Pacific Railroad land grant. The new owners would not divulge how much they paid for the property, but before Plum Creek completed the sale, Oregon businessman Tim Blixseth claimed he was willing to buy it for $6.5 million.

Both Poole and Vujovich invested a great deal of time and money drawing up plans that they feel will be both profitable to them and sensitive to the natural features of the area. They studied reports from former state wildlife biologist John Cada, fishery biologist Joe Urbani, forester Gary Peck, and hydrologists Tom and Trina Kallenbach. Their plans call for major development, including ski lifts, high-priced subdivisions, and a small commercial village. Three subdivisions, one of which is linked to the planned ski area and commercial village, are located at the head of Jack Creek. Two major parcels, a 4,100-acre tract and a 2,850-acre tract located at the other end of the road, are to be sold to conservation buyers—people who either won't develop the land or will severely restrict development. The remaining portion of the area, 11,000 acres or nearly half of Jack Creek, will be placed in conservation easements to protect the watershed and wildlife habitat.

Prior to the project, conservationists had ongoing concerns that this secluded area would be inundated with human traffic. Ennis business owners once lobbied for government funds to turn the narrow, dirt logging road running through the drainage into a paved public thoroughfare linking Ennis to the booming Big Sky resort. This disturbed environmentalists, who feared major disruption of elk migration routes and grizzly bear habitat. Under current plans, the privately financed road will remain closed to the public. Only owners of lots in the subdivisions will be allowed to use it. Electronic gatehouses at both ends of the road will control entry.

To date, property sales have gone very well. Twenty-two lots of twenty acres each in the Ulerys Lakes subdivision went on the market at an asking price of between $185,000 and $265,000. Within eighteen months, all lots were sold. Five lots of twenty acres each in the Timber Ridge subdivision went on the market for between $275,000 and $285,000. After fourteen months, four were sold. Diamond Hitch, the third subdivision, contains forty-seven one-acre lots, which will be served by two ski lifts. Moonlight Basin Ranch owners have taken contracts for seven of the forty-seven one-acre lots in the Diamond Hitch subdivision, which range in price from $175,000 to $295,000. And one of the large conservation tracts was sold in April 1994 for an undisclosed price to a couple from New York.

Again, the enviro-capitalists are taking care of the environment because they can contract for the sale of the amenities. Opposition from local residents and environmentalists has subsided. Bart Koehler of the Greater Yellowstone Coalition, a Montana-based environmental group, thinks the owners "deserve a lot of credit for putting forth a thoughtful and wildlife-sensitive plan for how their holdings are going to be managed in the future." "I think we're lucky," says Bill Murdock, director of the Big Sky Owners Association. "Someone else could have purchased it, and it would be a whole different ball game."[2] This did not happen because entrepreneurship and profits are on the side of Big Sky and the environment.

The View from Eagle Rock

The large commercial resort at Big Sky is one of several examples of eco-developers in Montana's Gallatin Valley. Within a few miles of Bozeman, a buyer can pick from a variety of developments with names like Bridger Creek Ranch, Triple Tree Ranch, or Sun West Ranch. All provide property owners with an assortment of natural amenities, including trout streams, hiking trails, and wildlife habitat. However, not all are as sensitive to the environment as Eagle Rock Reserve.

Eagle Rock, the idea of Bill F. Ogden Jr., a financial consultant, lawyer, and nature lover, takes its cue from barons of preservation (see chapter 2). Family members on his wife's side have belonged to the Huron Mountain Club in northern Michigan for many years, and Ogden is hoping to repeat Huron Mountain Club's 106-year-old success story by applying a similar concept to the Eagle Rock development. Like Huron Mountain Club, Eagle Rock combines limited residential use with the preservation of a large tract of land containing natural amenities. Although Ogden is committed to the project's financial success, he is also committed to bringing together people who "care about the earth" and want to spend time "living in harmony with beautiful natural surroundings."[3] He elects not to advertise in traditional real estate outlets, preferring instead to rely on publications such as *Audubon* and *Fly Fisherman*.

To say that the 774-acre reserve is conveniently located would be an understatement. Less than ten minutes from the front gate of the reserve is downtown Bozeman, Montana—one of the fastest-growing cities in the state. At the reserve's back door are several million acres of forests, mountains, streams, rivers, and lakes that make up part of the Greater Yellowstone ecosystem. Eagle Rock Reserve is actually a microcosm of Montana's natural bounty. It includes ranching, horseback riding, trout fishing, wildlife viewing, hiking, and beautiful mountain scenery. As the advertising brochure explains, "Your homesite is private, uncrowded, backing on the greater Yellowstone Wilderness. You have the vast common lands of prairie shared with hawks, eagles, and falcons. Timber and draws filled with chokecherry and snowberry provide cover for elk, deer, and birds. Here you can ride horses over the bunch grass prairies and wildflowers of arrowleaf balsam, lupine, and bluebells."[4]

Ogden selected home sites before the lots went on the market to ensure that they blended into the natural surroundings. The reserve's private road system follows ridge lines while each home site is tucked into the valleys, out of sight of other homes. In fact, from a distance, the development looks undeveloped. The buyer of a parcel at Eagle Rock purchases twenty acres but retains only three acres for his residential area; the other seventeen acres become part of the 650 acres of common easement area. This means 90 percent of the Eagle Rock property is dedicated to open space and wildlife habitat. Upon the project's completion, thirty-nine three-acre residential sites will be on the reserve. Owners who wish to keep horses can use a common saddling barn and stable as well as the common pasture. Every property owner pays an annual fee to the Eagle Rock Property Owners' Association, which has overall responsibility for managing and maintaining the reserve's open space, wildlife habitat, and road system. The association employs a full-time resident manager.

Resident wildlife is a key selling point for Eagle Rock's conservation-minded residents. The reserve provides important winter range and calving areas for between 40 and 130 elk that frequent the property. Other resident wildlife includes moose, bear, white-tailed and mule deer, and dozens of smaller mammals and birds. Hunting is not allowed on the reserve itself, but residents can find plenty of hunting opportunities within easy walking distance on nearby national and state forests. The wildlife share the reserve's forage with horses and cattle from neighboring ranches. The owners' association receives a grazing fee from the cattle owners and sells hay from the land, thereby reducing the risk of fire from dry grass.

The reserve has extensive covenants assuring residents that the amenities will remain protected. Beyond the requirements for open space and unobstructed views, these covenants include strict enforcement of architectural design and landscaping rules that ensure compatibility with the natural surroundings. Ogden understands that these contractual relationships between developer and home buyer are necessary to maintain the "natural harmony and ecology of the reserve."

As with any new product, the marketplace will provide the ultimate test for this environmentally aggressive approach. Even at the initial asking prices of $90,000 to $115,000 per lot, the development is out of the price range of local families, whose median income is $25,000 (1993 dollars). The developer is hoping that Eagle Rock will prove attractive to out-of-state professionals who want to retire to Bozeman or own a second home with outdoor amenities. Given the rate at which lots are selling and homes are being built at Eagle Rock, it appears that this enviro-capitalist is doing well while doing good.

Within sight of the Eagle Rock Reserve is another development that serves a different segment of the amenity market at a lower price. The 660-acre Triple Tree Ranch offers three-acre lots for $45,000 each, a price that compares favorably with nearby subdivision lots selling for $25,000 to $30,000.[5] At Triple Tree, Mike Potter, the developer, chose to leave roughly 330 acres of the ranch in open space, most of which is arranged as buffer zones between clusters of houses. Such an arrangement provides space and security for wildlife.

Missing from this development, however, is a large, contiguous block of open space that state biologists believe would be better for elk that winter in area. This is something the Eagle Rock developer could provide with the higher-priced parcels, but such preservation is more than the average home buyer could afford. The fragmented open space of Triple Tree allows the developer to create more lots—nearly three times as many as Eagle Rock—at a much lower price.

Eco-developers have responded to the demand for combined conservation and residential real estate in other areas of the country as well. In the early 1970s, for example, Forbes Inc., the publisher of *Forbes* magazine, acquired the gigantic Trinchera Ranch that stretches across 400 square miles of southern Colorado. Subsequently sold, the ranch's new ownership has continued Trinchera's tradition of protecting a vast private wilderness area that is home to abundant elk, deer, bear, grouse, wild turkey, and waterfowl. Forbes's subsidiary, Sangre de Cristo Ranches, has sold residential sites of varying sizes on selected areas of the ranch to people seeking vacation or retirement homes with access rights to Trinchera's common lands. Similarly, the Ausable Club in Michigan, Phantom Canyon Ranch in Colorado, and Sea Ranch in California combine residential living with exclusive rights to large, privately owned open spaces with abundant wildlife and other natural amenities. All in all, wherever natural amenities are available for the packaging and a demand for them exists in the marketplace, eco-developers are responding.[6]

These housing developments illustrate a diversity of products. Each eco-developer's product differs according to the amount of open space, the recreational opportunities, the number of lots, and the price. More environmental sensitivity comes at a higher cost, one that not all buyers can afford. These developers are serving different markets and are providing varying amenity packages just as the automobile market serves diverse markets from Mercedes to Chevies.

The Mouse That Restored

Like most commercial developments, Disney's theme parks do not normally conjure up images of pristine environments but rather provoke significant opposition, as did the one proposed in the Shenandoah Valley, Virginia. Nevertheless, restoring and enhancing an important nature preserve in Florida is the byproduct of Disney's extravaganza at Disney World. In 1993 the Walt Disney Company purchased 8,500 acres of "prime wetlands and upland habitat" (Nature Conservancy 1994). Another 3,000 acres were donated by the Greater Orlando Aviation Authority to establish the Disney Wilderness Preserve (Nature Conservancy 1995).

The preserve is located forty miles south of Orlando in the headwaters of the Everglades. It is a mosaic of Florida's native plant communities. Pine flatwoods, scrubby flatwoods, dry and wet prairies, freshwater marshes, and forested wetlands harbor more than 160 animal species, including endangered bald eagles, Florida grasshopper sparrows, woodstorks, and the threatened Florida scrub jays, crested caracaras, and eastern indigo snakes. The preserve has the distinction of hosting twelve active bald eagle nests, the greatest concentration in the southeastern states. It may eventually be home to the endangered Florida panthers and red-cockaded woodpeckers.

Formerly a working cattle ranch, the land making up most of the preserve was purchased by Disney after the state of Florida endorsed an innovative plan to donate the land to the Nature Conservancy with long-term financial support provided by Disney. Disney proposed it as an alternative to the usual ways of mitigating environmental impact anticipated from building Celebration, a residential community located in northwest Osceola County. In the past, mitigation efforts from residential and commercial developments in Florida have met with only limited success because they entailed destroying valuable upland habitat to create wetlands in an isolated, developed landscape. Because the Celebration residential community will affect 450 acres of wetlands, Disney suggested that rather than create an equivalent area of artificial wetlands on the Celebration site (the standard response for mitigating development impacts), it would purchase, restore, and provide for the management of the 8,500-acre Walker Ranch, noted for its prime wetland and upland habitat. Disney's financial commitment to the overall effort is substantial. It will pay all costs associated with the management of the preserve for the next twenty years and will give the Nature Conservancy $1 million to be invested and used as a permanent endowment to pay expenses after the year 2002. Carol Browner, then secretary of the Florida Department of Environmental Protection, recognized this as an opportunity to restore an entire community of unfragmented wetlands and heartily endorsed the Disney proposal.

One of the first items on the agenda for Disney and the conservancy will be to stabilize water flows to the area. In the 1960s, the Army Corps of Engineers altered the flow of the Kissimmee River, an important source of water for the wetlands on the property. Reductions in water levels combined with prior land uses damaged over 2,500 acres of wetlands and adversely affected surrounding uplands. Efforts to stabilize water flows and enhance current wetlands include the use of prescribed burns, the filling of ditches, and the removal of other manmade structures that inhibit water flows to the wetlands.

As owner and manager of the preserve, the Nature Conservancy's mission will be to restore damaged areas, protect resident endangered species, and conduct environmental education. It is estimated that about 490 acres of impacted wetlands need to be restored, and another, less altered 1,470 acres need to be enhanced. Also, "Unlike conventional mitigation, the preserve will have an active public use and environmental education component," says Jora Young, director of the Nature Conservancy's science and education program. Young notes that there will be hands-on activities for the public and scientists who will encourage greater understanding of Florida's native lands (Nature Conservancy 1993, 2). This partnership represents a revolutionary approach to environmental mitigation. According to John Flicker, vice president of the conservancy's Florida chapter, "partnerships and solutions like this one will be essential in protecting Florida's ecology and economy" (Nature Conservancy 1994, 3).

Eco-Nondevelopers

Grassroots environmentalists often have very different means and ends than their big brothers in Washington. Like true entrepreneurs, these groups identify specific parcels of land they want to preserve and find cooperative methods for achieving their goals. Using this approach, grassroots local land trusts have protected 3 million acres nationwide in cooperation with private landowners.[7]

Land trust operators require skills to preserve these lands that resemble those of the developers more than of environmental advocacy groups. Land trust entrepreneurs must be innovative, sensitive to the needs of landowners, knowledgeable of the real estate market, and aware of innovative contracting. Typically a land trust representative identifies a land preservation parcel and devises a plan amenable to the landowner's needs. Because their goal is not to own all sticks in the landowner's bundle of rights, land trust entrepreneurs identify those aspects of the land's use that they want to control and purchase or obtain a donation of those sticks for the land trust. In either case, rights received by the land trust are usually held as conservation easements that restrict what can be done with the land. When rights are purchased, the benefit to the landowner is clear and direct; when rights are donated, the benefit accrues from a tax deduction for the difference between the value of the property with and without a conservation easement attached. Despite quid pro quo for the landowner, the land trust entrepreneur must still be innovative. Land conservation consultant John B. Wright says, "Rural ranchers go ballistic if you mention environmentalism. But if you scratch off the first layer of culture, you will discover that most of them care a lot about the land" (quoted in Larmer 1994, 10).

The Montana Land Reliance provides one example of many land trusts effectively gaining the goodwill of landowners. "Our goal is to help preserve a lifestyle and an economy that rely on responsibly managed private lands," says Amy O'Herren, director of the reliance's Kalispell office (quoted in Hansen-Malchik 1995). The Montana Land Reliance has already accomplished a great deal. From 1978 through 1993, it helped landowners protect over 120,000 acres of private land in Montana, mostly through the donation of conservation easements that are compatible with the needs of agriculture (Montana Land Reliance 1994). Under the reliance's conservation easement program, easements can even be designed to be saleable and transferable. Thus, if agricultural use is no longer economical for a specific parcel of land, the easement can be extinguished by the landowner by buying it back from the reliance. The reliance can then use the proceeds to secure an easement on other land. This approach recognizes that land use change may become necessary but maintains the overall preservation goal by shifting amenity protection to other parcels.

Taking a cue from local land trusts, some environmental activist groups are finding that working with landowners to provide less disruptive development can avoid landowner resentment emanating from a regulatory approach. Pamela Lichtman of the Jackson Hole Alliance for Responsible Planning in Wyoming says her organization has achieved more success protecting wildlife habitat on private lands with this approach than by lobbying for tougher zoning laws. Says Lichtman, "This is a new area for us. We take people's own benevolence and sense of sacrifice and work with them to protect the valley's natural resources" (quoted in Larmer 1994, 10).

Some nonprofit entrepreneurs are even willing to invest in the design and development of partial development projects to protect natural amenities. In the early 1980s, two entrepreneurs with Colorado Open Lands (COL), a nonprofit, "public purpose" corporation, took this approach to save an ecologically valuable property from intensive development. The focus of their effort was the Evans Ranch, a 3,200-acre livestock operation located forty miles west of Denver. Bounded on three sides by public lands, it is home to a great diversity of wildlife, including a wintering herd of 300 elk. The proximity of the ranch to Denver, abundant wildlife, spectacular mountain landscape, and its importance to Colorado history make this land unique even in a state with abundant Rocky Mountain amenities.

The property was assembled in the 1860s by Colorado's second territorial governor, John Evans. His heirs continued to own the property in a trust arrangement that required the property to generate income for the family. Until 1980 this income came from cattle ranching. However, in that year, change was in the wind as suburban sprawl began to envelop the ranch at a time when cattle ranching was becoming less profitable. Situated only forty-five minutes from Denver, the property had numerous developers champing at the bit to develop it. And under the county zoning laws at the time, the option of subdividing the ranch into 1,600 two-acre lots seemed inevitable.

In 1981, COL entered the picture. COL was staffed by two very different but capable individuals, Marty Zeller, a planner with an M.A. from Harvard, and Don Walker, a baseball player from the University of Colorado. The Colorado Forum, an association of chief executive officers from twenty-five major corporations operating in the state, formed COL to preserve open space along Colorado's Front Range, where population growth was three times the national average. COL also assembled a board of directors with several successful development entrepreneurs, including the presidents of two large real estate development corporations, Mission Viejo and Inverness. When COL was founded as nonprofit, the outlook for local funding seemed bleak because declining oil and gas prices had sent Colorado into a recession. Walker recognized that COL had to explore approaches that would enable it to become self-supporting.

To launch the open-space preservation drive, Don Walker wanted a successful project that would become a centerpiece reflecting what could be accomplished with entrepreneurial approaches. The impending sale of the Evans Ranch provided the perfect candidate. Unfortunately, the price tag on the ranch was a hefty $4,665,000. The family wanted to conserve as much of the land as possible but also was desperate for funds and under a court order to liquidate the property.

The COL board and staff decided partial development could provide a way of meeting the family's requirements. Lacking enough cash to make a 10 percent down payment on the ranch, COL offered to purchase a one-year option on the ranch's 3,200 acres for $5,000. Pressured by the Evans family, the bank holding the note on the ranch agreed to COL's seemingly desperate plan. In twelve months, however, the young organization needed to make a down payment of $445,000 or lose its initial investment and the prospect of preservation.

COL was serious about designing a sensitive plan for saving the ranch's amenities. The staff turned to planner Ian McHarg from Philadelphia, best known as the author of *Design With Nature*, a book that influenced an entire generation of planners and conservationists. After a few months, McHarg and the COL staff completed a plan called "Stewards of the Valley." Under the plan, the property would be divided into five individual ranches of 640 acres. Each ranch would have a thirty-five-acre building area with the remainder set aside as permanent open space protected by restrictive covenants held by COL. Every owner would have the right to use the entire open-space acreage for recreation within the original property. The price for each of the five ranches was $1.5 million.

By the time the "Stewards of the Valley" plan was in place, the first payment on COL's option was coming due, and the organization's funds were dwindling. Walker and Zeller approached the Gates Foundation in Denver for a $5,000 contribution to cover the day-to-day expenses of the organization. To their surprise, the Gates Foundation made a counteroffer. According to Walker, the foundation agreed to loan COL the money for any payments they could not make on the Evans Ranch. If they could not make payments, Gates would own the land. With no collateral, Walker and Zeller had obtained a $4.7 million loan guarantee (see Walker and Zeller 1990, 15).

The Gates Foundation, however, never had to write any checks because in 1982 three of the five smaller ranches sold, netting $4 million after the down payment of $445,000 was made to the bank. By 1987, the last two ranches were sold, and the Evans property was permanently protected. Walker and Zeller's bold project paid off handsomely with $3 million going into COL's endowment fund.

Land trusts and unique organizations like COL still face many more challenges. With the demand for recreational and commercial property escalating throughout the West, a good deal of chutzpah and financial backing are required to compete in the marketplace. The latter may come from private grant-making foundations willing to take the same chance the Gates Foundation took, but entrepreneurs like Walker and Zeller will have to provide the innovative ideas and contracts.

Rearranging the Bundle of Sticks

Eco-developers and nondevelopers alike require a legal environment in which they can easily contract to recombine sticks in the bundle of rights held by landowners. There may be physical investments such as the trout streams made by Peter O'Neill, but it is generally the rearrangement of rights that creates value. For example, Bill Ogden added value to Eagle Rock by rearranging the sticks in the bundle of rights to each twenty-acre lot. Rather than selling each owner in the development the right to do as he or she pleased with twenty acres, he withheld the stick that allowed a homeowner to build anywhere and required rights to most of the land be transferred back to the commons. This freedom of contract is the essence of enviro-capitalism.

When the freedom of contract is limited by zoning, taxes, or regulations, entrepreneurial visions may not be realized. Certainly Dayton Hyde's experience should be a red flag to all concerned with creating a legal regime hospitable to private protection of the environment. He tried to make investments in his property on which he could later capitalize by selling them to others. Limiting an entrepreneur's ability to profit from transferring property rights also limits the potential for creating environmental wealth. As people are willing to pay more to live with wild things, entrepreneurs have an incentive to find innovative ways of making development compatible with those wild things. Allowing and encouraging eco-developers to rearrange the traditional bundle of property rights is a necessary step in the direction of compatibility. Where we go from here depends on the market for amenities and the institutional environment in which private landowners transact.

Notes

1. Telephone interview with Dayton Hyde, 1 August 1995.
2. Both are quoted in Ellig (1995).
3. Quoted from a brochure on Eagle Rock Reserve, Bozeman, Montana.
4. Quoted from a brochure on Eagle Rock Reserve, Bozeman, Montana.
5. Information available from Triple Tree Ranch headquartered in Bozeman, Montana.
6. For a more complete discussion, see Wolf (1995).
7. This total does not include the efforts of nonprofit groups with a national scope, such as the Nature Conservancy and the American Farmland Trust.

References

Ellig, Tracy. 1995. Partners Tout Moonlight Basin as 'A Privatized Version of a National Park.' *Bozeman Daily Chronicle*, February 5.

Hansen-Malchik, Laulette. 1995. A Piece of Forever. *Whitefish: The Magazine of Northwest Montana*, winter/spring.

Hyde, Dayton O. 1986. Recreation and Wildlife on Private Land. In *Recreation on Private Lands: Issues and Opportunities*. Washington, DC: Task Force on Recreation on Private Lands, 23–30.

Larmer, Paul. 1994. A Soft-Paths Approach to Land Conservation. *High Country News*, September 5.

Leopold, Aldo. 1971. Foreword. *A Sand County Almanac with Essays on Conservation from Round River*. Reprint. New York: Ballantine Books.

Montana Land Reliance. 1994. 1993—A Record-Breaking Year for MLR. *Montana Land Reliance News*. Helena, MT: Montana Land Reliance, spring.

Nature Conservancy. 1993. It's Official! Conservancy to Own and Manage 8,500-Acre Disney Wilderness Preserve. *Nature Conservancy*. Florida Chapter, spring.

———. 1994. From Real Estate to Real Solutions. *Natural Assets*, fall.

———. 1995. *The Disney Wilderness Preserve: 1995 Fact Sheet*. Kissimmee, FL: Nature Conservancy.

Smith, Robert J. 1984. Special Report: The Public Benefits of Private Conservation. *Environmental Quality, 15th Annual Report of the Council on Environmental Quality*. Washington DC: Council on Environmental Quality, 363–429.

Walker, Donald V. H., and Martin E. Zeller. 1985. Promoting Public/Private Initiatives for Preservation. *Urban Land*, November.

Wolf, Thomas J. 1995. The Capitalist Tool: Wildlife Management in Colorado's Sangre de Cristo Mountains. In *Wildlife in the Marketplace*, ed. Terry L. Anderson and Peter J. Hill. Lanham, MD: Rowman and Littlefield Publishers, 127–45.

Chapter 7

Going Global

When it comes to salmon recovery, there are no problems, only opportunities.

— Orri Vigfusson
Atlantic Salmon Federation

Like species in the wild, entrepreneurs require a special environment that allows them to thrive. Secure property rights, sufficient wealth to afford environmental protection, and the rule of law are necessary conditions to foster contracts that produce long-term investments in the natural environment. Most of the examples presented in the first six chapters came from the United States, where the legal environment provides these conditions. From Peter O'Neill's home-grown amenity projects in Idaho that harmonize fish and wildlife needs with residential development to Ted Turner's ranch rehabilitation projects that combine conservation easements, fee hunting, stream doctoring, and bison production, enviro-capitalists seeking returns on long-term investments in amenities can only capture those returns in an economic system that allows people to reap what they sow.

However, the United States is not the only place where enviro-capitalists can find the economic and institutional environment that fosters amenity investment and innovation. From England to South Africa, the demand for amenities is growing as incomes increase. Entrepreneurs have responded by investing in the environment, and the natural world is better off. To stop a forty-year decline in Britain's butterfly populations, the private, nonprofit British Butterfly Conservation Society records and monitors sites with important butterfly populations and, when possible, acquires them to ensure long-term protection. Entrepreneurs Varty and Bernstein have guided Conservation Corporation to its place as Africa's premier eco-tourism company. In so doing, they have benefited investors and wildlife alike. And Orri Vigfusson, vodka dealer and Atlantic salmon lover, has assisted with the recovery of wild Atlantic salmon stocks by purchasing netting rights from commercial fishermen. The radar of these entrepreneurs is switched on both by environmental ethics and by profits, the latter requiring security of title. Each case offers another experiment with new contracts and new marketing techniques. But perhaps more importantly, these examples from other countries offer fascinating comparisons of how different legal regimes encourage or thwart enviro-capitalists.

The examples that follow come from countries sharing a common legal heritage that depends on the rule of law and respects private property rights. In the absence of this legal environment, incentives disappear, and stewardship suffers. Like other assets, the natural environment will only be protected if the people who must invest in it can reap rewards. As the Iron Curtain fell in eastern Europe, it became clear that communism was not hospitable to investment in environmental quality because it did not generate wealth, encourage private initiative, or provide future security. The lesson is that development and survival of a global species of enviro-capitalists depends as much on security of tenure as it does on entrepreneurial vision. These international examples shed light on the institutional requirements necessary to foster a global species of enviro-capitalists.

The Corporate Jungle

"We are asking companies to invest in conservation, not to donate to it," says Dave Varty, cofounder of Conservation Corporation (Conscorp), a South African company started in 1990. Varty and deputy chairman Alan Bernstein make no apologies for the fact that they are trying to turn a profit from wildlife (quoted in Luhsche 1995). To the contrary, they, along with many other conservationists in southern Africa, believe that profits are the key to ensuring the survival of both wildlife and its habitat.

Varty and Bernstein combined their respective eco-tourism and financial skills to create one of the first, large-scale businesses to invest in wildlife conservation. Prior to forming Conscorp, Varty owned Londolozi Reserve, one of South Africa's most successful commercial private wildlife ranches, and Bernstein was managing director of a company that raised money for investment in sub-Saharan Africa. As of 1995, the partners had raised $40 million[1] and had plans for a $20 million expansion project. In addition to Londolozi, Conscorp opened Phinda Reserve, which comprised 17,000 hectares of private land; negotiated an innovative contract with Kruger National Park that incorporates the 14,000-hectare Ngala private reserve on the western boundary into the park while giving Conscorp exclusive operating rights; and established the 15,000-hectare Singita Reserve, where the "Big Five" (elephant, rhinoceros, Cape buffalo, lion, and leopard) can be seen.[2] The corporation is also diversifying beyond its initial four game lodges in South Africa by planning a new 49,000-hectare game reserve near Victoria Falls in Zimbabwe.

It took four years to start the flow of black ink, but these two envirocapitalists have every expectation of riding the rising tide of eco-tourism in Africa. Conscorp's net operating loss fell from nearly $1 million in 1993 to less than $200,000 in 1994, and they turned a profit in 1995. Their financial picture was not helped by concerns that the 1994 elections in South Africa might result in violence. Hence, occupancy levels at Conscorp lodges in South Africa averaged only 50 percent in 1993 and 1994. Relative political stability, however, increased occupancy rates at Londolozi Lodge to near capacity and at the Ngala and Phinda Forest Lodges to over 70 percent in 1995. Bernstein says that Conscorp is "experiencing unprecedented levels of demand," causing weekly booking income to rise fivefold in 1995 (quoted in Luhsche 1995).

Game lodges and hunting are nothing new in South Africa, where game ranching is the "fastest growing and most dynamic livestock industry," according to Andrew Conroy, chairman of the National Game Organization (Conroy 1992). Game ranching competes effectively with domestic livestock and thus sustains wildlife populations where they would be crowded out by cattle. In Conroy's view, the variety of production methods and the biological diversity encouraged by the industry is unprecedented anywhere in the world. There are about 50,000 local hunters and 400 professional hunters in the country. In addition, more than 4,000 foreign hunters visit South Africa every year. Approximately $100 million of income is generated each year from game farming by way of fee hunting, live sales of animals, tourism, and sales of venison and other game products.

The value of wildlife in the marketplace is indicated by the prices paid for live animals at auctions. In Hluhluwe, South Africa, an auction of antelopes, giraffes, zebras, and rhinos brought $1.4 million on 1 July 1995. Of course, the seventy rhinos brought the highest prices. For example, a white rhino bull captured by the Natal Parks Board using a helicopter and tranquilizer dart brought $20,000. Bulls like this one with trophy-length horns were being sold to private reserves where hunters will pay as much as $30,000 for chance to shoot a trophy. The rarer black rhinos cannot be hunted, but they bring even higher prices from breeders wanting to establish herds for viewing and for future sale. When the hammer fell on a breeding herd of six black rhinos sold in one lot, the price was $40,000 per animal. As George Hughes of the Natal Parks Board, which uses the proceeds from sales to maintain its game reserves, put it, "If wildlife can pay for itself, it has a better chance of staying" (quoted in McDowell 1995). At $40,000 each, the rhinos have an excellent chance of being around for a while.

Though wildlife ranching is not new to South Africa, the innovative contracting that Conscorp uses to make wildlife pay is. The corporation generally owns only small land parcels, enough to accommodate its lodges. For the rest, Conscorp contracts with surrounding landowners for conservation services. Rather than tying up capital in vast tracts, Conscorp has contracted for access to private lands for game viewing and hunting.

Consider the articles of association that Conscorp developed to contract with private landowners when it formed the Mun-Ya-Wana Game Reserve in South Africa's northern Transvaal province.[3] Mun-Ya-Wana encompasses 30,000 hectares. The articles state that some purposes of the reserve are, among others, "to promote and conserve endemic wildlife and habitat within the confines of the area . . . ; to establish the Reserve as a sanctuary in perpetuity for endemic wildlife and habitat so as to enable sustainable resource utilization . . . ; to endeavor to increase the area of the Reserve . . . ;" and "to maximize the long-term economic and ecological value of the properties. . . ." Above all, the company tries to minimize congestion because "large numbers of persons on the Reserve are undesirable."

Because Conscorp is catering to tourists who want to enjoy game in the natural African bush, the company strives to keep all development on the reserve "congruent with the principle of minimal environmental impact and minimal aesthetic impact." Road use is strictly limited to those specified in the articles of association. Game drives must avoid residential areas and are coordinated through a radio network, with each member responsible for erecting and maintaining a base station. The company controls the number of game drive vehicles and boats to avoid congestion problems. The architecture of all structures erected on the reserve must be "ecologically and aesthetically sympathetic," and "the siting of structures and services on and to the reserve are placed in unobtrusive places so as not to have an adverse effect on the surroundings." To promote wildlife and maintain a natural setting, landowners agree not to keep domestic animals, including dogs and cats. They can build structures on their property but only with written consent from the company and only after submitting detailed drawing and artists impressions. To maintain the integrity of the reserve, landowners cannot subdivide their properties and cannot undertake other commercial activities such as prospecting or establishing tent villages or caravan parks without agreement from the company.

Why would landowners be willing to agree to include their lands in the reserve given all of these restrictions? In a word, profits. Conscorp estimates that dry land cattle ranching earns approximately $21 per hectare per year, and cropping earns $68. This compares to nearly $200 to $300 per hectare per year in Conscorp reserves. This explains the landowners' interest in negotiating contracts with Messrs. Bernstein and Varty. Howard Geach, Conscorp marketing director, says, "We are demonstrating a form of land use involving wildlife as a sort of cash crop" (quoted in Koch 1995).

The perimeters of Conscorp properties are fenced with an eight-foot-high game fence made of twelve strands of high-tensile, smooth wire, but game within cannot be "tethered or enclosed in any cage or fence" and "irrespective of that game's ownership, shall be entitled to graze, browse, or feed anywhere on a reserve." To guarantee that animals cannot leave the reserve, each landowner is responsible for erecting a perimeter fence meeting company standards for the land under his control. Maintenance of the fence is the responsibility of the company. To ensure the most natural setting and to guarantee free range for the animals, the landowner must "lift and remove the fences which surround or traverse his land, save where the fence in question is a perimeter fence . . . or a protection fence immediately adjacent to a dwelling." The company erects gates and garrison guards at the gates to control access.

Because game is free to move anywhere on the reserve, Conscorp has written a very detailed contract specifying the rules for culling, hunting, and capturing. Before a prospective landowner is admitted into the company, a census of the number and species of game on the property is conducted. If the census shows that the landowner's game populations are insufficient to contribute to the overall purposes, "then the prospective member shall be obliged to supplement the species, in kind or in cash as may be agreed with the Company." Each year, another census is conducted to determine net changes in game populations, and the company allocates "proportionally to each land controller the overall increase or decrease in game numbers. . . ." Any disagreements over numbers are arbitrated by the state wildlife agency known as the parks board, and the board's decisions are final and binding on all parties. Members are not allowed to introduce any new species to the reserve without prior written consent of the company, but the company may withhold consent only if the species is not indigenous to the region. The company can also introduce species, which then become the property of the company. The agreement allows landowners to "cull, hunt, or capture game" provided the activities follow the laws, regulations, and rules of the parks board, and provided the landowner obtains a permit from the company specifying the number of game to be taken. Any member who did not contribute any of a particular species to the collective herd is not entitled "to hunt, cull, or claim ownership or benefit from the proceeds of any sale of that specie[s] except where a separate agreement is in place." Hunting, culling, or capturing must take place within the landowner's boundaries. If an injured animal escapes to land controlled by another, "only the leader of the hunt and one tracker may follow the specie of game in question onto the land of another member in accordance with the rules laid down from time to time."

The company makes special provisions for the introduction of a species, such as the rhinoceros, for trophy hunting. Again, the animal cannot be prevented from ranging over the reserve, but when it wanders onto land controlled by another, "the landowners will be obliged to agree on a method of resolving this problem and allowing the owner of the introduced animal to hunt the animal on the property where it has moved to. In the event that the parties cannot agree it will fall upon the disciplinary committee of the directors or failing that the directors to rule as a matter of urgency in this matter to achieve a speedy solution."

Enviro-capitalists Varty and Bernstein typify what can be done with entrepreneurial vision, venture capital, and innovative contracting. By combining Varty's land management skills with Bernstein's financial prowess, Conscorp has overcome the "transaction costs" that economists often argue limit the ability of the market to produce environmental amenities. The articles of association for Mun-Ya-Wana Game Reserve show what private contracting can do.

Net-Free Salmon

The United States is losing the battle to restore wild Atlantic salmon runs to New England rivers despite over $35 million spent, mostly by the government, restoring the water quality and restocking rivers. The big reason why wild salmon on the Atlantic coast are not returning is that many are lost to the commercial nets of fishermen off the southwest coast of Greenland and Faroe Islands, where the salmon feed and grow before returning to spawn in their native rivers.

Stopping commercial salmon fishing, even temporarily, would be difficult. Because salmon are the main source of income for Greenland and Faroe Islands fishermen, they are unwilling to simply give up netting on the high seas. Thus, the obvious question is what can be done to alleviate the income loss for these fishermen if salmon netting is stopped. One enviro-capitalist from Iceland has a promising answer.

Orri Vigfusson decided to circumvent the bureaucratic, regulatory approach with a proposal that allows both sport and commercial fishermen to win if netting is reduced. When this Icelandic businessman is not distilling and exporting vodka, he is either sport fishing for Atlantic salmon, raising them at his aquafarm, or seeking to restore wild stocks. He began in 1987 by investing his own resources in a study that established a link between netting and declining salmon stocks. Working from his salmon farm on the Laxa River in northeast Iceland, researchers tagged 8,000 fish and released them into the open ocean. The tagged fish did not return to spawn, but their tags were returned to Vigfusson by fishermen from Greenland and the Faroe Islands who caught the fish in their nets. This evidence convinced Vigfusson, a director of the Atlantic Salmon Federation (ASF), that it was netting that prevented salmon from returning to spawn and hence was putting stocks at risk.

In 1989, to combat the problem of overfishing, Vigfusson took a page from the water broker's book (see chapter 5) and developed a proposal to retire commercial salmon quotas held by fishermen in Greenland and the Faroe Islands. The ASF gave full support to Vigfusson's buyout plan and began raising funds immediately. In 1991, an agreement was reached with Faroe Islands fishermen to compensate them for not exercising netting rights in 1991, 1992, and 1993. Just as farmers receive payments not to irrigate, the Faroe Islands fishermen received $685,500 per year not to fish. As a result, in 1993, nearly twice as many salmon returned to their native rivers in Iceland and Europe. In the same year, Vigfusson temporarily bought out netting rights of fishermen in Greenland for 1993 and 1994. The deal paid fishermen $400,000 each year and reduced salmon netting off Greenland from 213 metric tons to 12 metric tons (Scott 1993).

Though a small quota remains to support a subsistence fishery for the Inuit tribe, sufficient netting rights have been retired to augment salmon stocks. The long-term goal of Vigfusson and the salmon federation is to establish a compensation plan that will completely eliminate ocean salmon netting off Greenland and the Faroe Islands. This program would compensate fishermen for the income they forgo from the projected catch and would finance training programs for fishermen that would prepare them for other work.

Vigfusson believes that a program that retires netting rights and retrains fishermen will be better for them in the long run because they will be attaining skills capable of providing a sustainable occupation. Moreover, the inland salmon fisheries have the potential to produce additional economic wealth from recreational fishing. "While the value of one salmon is about $15 for a commercial fisherman, that same fish is probably worth $1,000 if it feeds into the sport of line fishing and associated commercial activity. And that can only happen if the fish return home to spawn" (quoted in Weintraub 1993, 82).

Orri Vigfusson is able to apply his entrepreneurial skills to the North Atlantic salmon problem because the legal environment has established a system of transferable netting rights over which Vigfusson and the fishermen can contract.

Down on the Farm

The cold North Atlantic fosters another breed of enviro-capitalists who have been farming eider (a large sea-dwelling duck) for down and eggs for more than two centuries. The use of eider by-products dates as far back as the first settlement of Iceland in A.D. 874, while eider protection is documented as far back as the thirteenth century. In 1230, the owner of an island near Reykjavik and a local priest agreed not to kill eiders. This agreement indicates that locals valued eiders and wanted them protected from excessive exploitation. In 1281, civil and ecclesiastical codes spelled out the protection of eiders, noting that they were to be "unmolested within 240 spans of their nesting places, and each farmer was instructed not to catch too many ducks" (Doughty 1979, 344).

In the late eighteenth century, the stage was set to move away from eider hunting and toward eider farming. In 1787, the Danish parliament issued a list of protective measures for the colony of Iceland. The list included the prohibition of eider harvesting except on one's own land. Even a decade prior to the parliamentary edict, people like agriculturist and industrialist Skuli Magnusson were busy promoting the concept of protecting and farming the nesting places of eiders for down and eggs. In the 1770s, Magnusson harvested down and eggs from eider nests and husbanded a very large colony of eiders on the island of Videy. Historical accounts document that he collected about ninety pounds of down from his "favorite" birds (Doughty 1979, 346). Because fines for illegal eider hunting were weakly enforced, a bill signed by the Danish king in 1849 made eider hunting illegal under any circumstances. The same bill extended property rights to eider down and eggs to the owners of land upon which eiders reside. With property rights secure, eider farming expanded.

Eider farming grew and reached a peak in the second decade of the twentieth century. Between 1909 and 1917, more than 250 farms supplied between 6,700 and 11,500 pounds of down annually (Doughty 1979, 346). Since World War II, production of down decreased to approximately half that amount, but some farmers continue to husband and protect the birds. They defend against poachers and predators, improve habitat, and even build artificial nesting sites. As a result, Iceland boasts some of the largest eider duck colonies in the world. Arni Snaebjoernsson, a specialist on eiders in Iceland, estimates the eider population there at 600,000 to 900,000 birds.

Eider farming remains an important economic activity, with exports ranging between 1.5 and 3.2 tons of down a year. According to the Icelandic Association of Eiderduck Farmers, approximately one hundred farmers derive a considerable part of their income from the collection of down from eiders. For example, Baldur Bjarnason and his family farm Vigur Island, where 4,000 nesting pairs of eiders produce enough down to constitute 60 percent of the family's annual income. Says Bjarnason, "It's like raising sheep for their wool" (Hyman 1982, 6). His annual harvest is approximately 114 pounds. If he sells this amount at $234 to $315 per pound,[4] the range of wholesale prices from 1988 to 1993, Bjarnason would gross $26,500 to $36,000 per year in U.S. dollars.

Financial and stewardship rewards also have come from farming other seabirds in Iceland. On Grimsley Island, off Iceland's north coast, Bjarni Magnusson harvests eggs from common murres, razorbills, and black-legged kittiwakes. Eight farms on the island harvest about 1,500 eggs per day from these birds, and the total harvest in a season is about 35,000 eggs. The eggs can bring $10 per dozen in the mainland towns. Farmers can sustain their harvest by taking eggs early in the nesting season because most birds will lay new eggs to replace those harvested (Hyman 1982, 8).

Down and egg farming in Iceland allows birds to receive the benefits of private stewardship. Like the other wild birds, eiders will nest only where they feel protected and undisturbed, and eider farms offer this security. Bjarnason and others have a vested interest in protecting nesting sites from intrusions because they know that this will ensure the return of eiders to their properties. Says Bjarnason, "If the eiders have success hatching their eggs one year, they always return the next. . . . Most of our ducks use the same nest sites year after year" (quoted in Hyman 1982, 6). In addition to keeping intruders away, the Bjarnasons are careful when and how they walk. Nesting mothers must not be prevented from returning to their nests, especially in the early mornings when they take their daily baths. Because females are so well camouflaged and densely grouped, the Bjarnasons are careful where they step lest they squash an unsuspecting mother.

Bread and Butterflies

During World War II, Great Britain's countryside changed dramatically as pastures and meadows that had survived for centuries were ploughed and cultivated for food production. Since the war, change has continued, as old-style farming techniques have gradually given way to more intensive agriculture. To make matters worse, governmental subsidies have encouraged farmers to convert would-be wildlife habitat to cropland and to make heavier use of pesticides, herbicides, and fertilizers.

One victim of these changes has been Britain's once-prolific butterfly populations. Today, Britain still has fifty-four resident butterfly species and a half-dozen that visit the island regularly from abroad. But twenty-three native species have been declared endangered, and another seven are on the verge of extinction.

The British Butterfly Conservation Society, a private, registered charity (nonprofit company) in the United Kingdom, is trying to halt this decline. The society was incorporated in 1968, and until 1990, was run entirely by volunteers. It now has an administrative headquarters, a full-time manager, and a full-time conservation officer, Dr. Martin Warren, appointed in 1993 to oversee research on woodlands butterflies. The society's president is the celebrated wildlife author, artist, and broadcaster Gordon Benington, elected in 1990 following the death of Sir Peter Scott, who held the position from the society's inception until his death.

The society is "the largest insect habitat conservation group in the world" (Phillips 1992, 6), with 10,000 members and twenty-six active regional branches. Members record and monitor butterflies and their habitat. When possible, the society's branches secure sites of particular value to butterflies by purchasing the properties, acquiring long-term leases, or establishing land use agreements with private owners. A British Butterfly Conservation Society brochure notes that the private ownership is seen as crucial to its mission: "Where possible we want to acquire sites of particular worth, for only through ownership can their future be truly assured" (Phillips 1992, 8). To date, the society's branches have established sixteen private reserves in the United Kingdom, ranging in size from the Little Breach Reserve, less than 1 hectare, to the Monkwood Reserve, 61.4 hectares (Kirkland n.d., 12). The most recently established reserve is Oaken Wood, which supports over thirty species, including Britain's rare wood white, pearl-bordered fritillary, and small pearl-bordered fritillary butterflies.

In addition to land acquisition, the society's branches carry out a host of other activities. They organize field trips, believing that such trips are the best way for beginners to learn about butterflies. Regional branches work out cooperative arrangements with other wildlife groups to educate the public on butterflies and their plight. The Beds and Northants Branch, for example, completed an agreement with the management of Whipsnade Wild Animal Park to create a butterfly garden. The branch sees the garden as an important educational tool and hopes it will inspire visitors to plant more butterfly-friendly gardens. The society also sponsors scientific research and encourages members to conduct their own research activities in an effort to learn more about individual butterfly species and to discover the most effective ways of protecting them. Research is critical to improving the status of butterflies because their life cycles and needs remain poorly understood.

The British Butterfly Conservation Society finances its activities through membership subscriptions, donations and grants from charitable foundations and corporations, and income generated from the society's numerous and informative publications. Its benefactors include charitable trusts such as the Vincent Wildlife Trust, the Alan Evans Memorial Trust, the Garfield Weston Foundation, and the Lady Hind Trust, and companies such as Land Rover, British Airways, Enterprise Oil, and Premier Consolidated Oilfields. For the fiscal year that ended 30 June 1994, the society collected approximately $550,000, generated from subscriptions, grants, donations, and publications, and about $1.7 million from interest on its endowment. In 1994, it spent nearly $220,000 on conservation projects, including the purchase of two reserves in public real estate auctions.[5]

Finders, Keepers

Looking across the British moor, hunters eagerly await the arrival of their winged quarry, the red grouse, a subspecies of the North American willow ptarmigan. The birds will be driven by a long line of energetic "beaters" who beat the ground with sticks and gunny sacks to flush the birds from their hiding places and into a flight path in front of the hunters. Alongside each hunter is a loader who provides shotgun shells as needed and, on not-too-infrequent occasions when the hunter misses the bird, a bit of shooting advice. The hunters pay handsomely for grouse hunting on a private British moor. For a day's shoot, eight hunters will pay upwards of $15,000 or $1,875 per person to the moor's owner.

Because landowners can profit from their bird populations, Britain's red grouse and other game birds are plentiful. Some of Britain's great Pennine moors can yield up to 250 or even 500 brace (a pair of birds shot) of grouse on a good August day. About 500,000 grouse are shot every year in Britain. Though this number pales in comparison to the 20 million pheasants shot each year, red grouse differ in that they are wild rather than pen-reared. In fact, "the grouse is the only species of animal that has been managed intensively and productively without being domesticated" (Ridley 1992, 34).

It is profits that preserve the tradition of wild grouse hunting, as well as the birds' wild, heather-filled moor habitat. Landowners control predators, provide the habitat, and hunt them to prevent the overpopulation that brings an inevitable onslaught of worms and parasites that can decimate a population. Guest fees provide most of the income, but as in South Africa, the sale of meat in local markets is also important. A small portion of the grouse killed in the day's hunt becomes dinner for the hunters, and the rest is sold to the hotels and restaurants in nearby towns for the night's dinner menus. Unfortunately, working against the profits from hunting are governmental subsidies for landowners who convert their moors to forests.

On the other hand, profits for moor owners are not just pecuniary. On one moor owned by a syndicate, for example, 1994 income, mostly from guest hunting fees and game sales, totaled nearly $120,000, while expenses, mainly salaries for gamekeepers, beaters, and security guards, was just over $125,000. A closer look at the numbers reveals that the owners sacrificed potential income from guest fees to hunt the moor, reserving eight days for themselves. At an average daily hunting income of nearly $15,000, the owners could have doubled their revenues and made a tidy profit by using their days for guest hunting. That they chose to hunt themselves suggests they valued their own hunting more than revenue.

The key to successful management of grouse and other game in Britain is the gamekeeper, whose tasks vary widely depending on the region.

> In the lowland areas, they are mainly concerned with breeding and protecting pheasants, partridges, and ducks. On higher ground, such as the heather moors, their job is to encourage a good stock of wild grouse. Further north, in the Scottish Highlands, gamekeepers or stalkers, as they are called, maintain herds of wild red deer that roam his employer's estate. (Alexander 1989, 35)

Colin Adamson, the gamekeeper for the wild grouse estate of Lord Biddulph, is one of 5,000 dedicated wildlife managers in Britain. In an article about gamekeepers in *International Wildlife*, Brian Alexander (1989) notes: "By maintaining habitat for game species, people like Adamson help preserve Britain's vital woodlands." Adamson is considered one of the best in the business for rearing grouse in the wild and providing hunters with high-quality shooting.

To ensure large grouse populations, gamekeepers must provide habitat for natural reproduction and control predators. Not surprisingly, predator control by gamekeepers is controversial. Some animal rights' groups oppose predator control on the grounds that it will upset the balance of the ecosystem, while others argue that gamekeepers illegally kill protected raptors. But Art Lance, director of the Royal Society for the Protection of Birds, concludes that the majority of British gamekeepers are conscientious and abide by laws that impose fewer restrictions on wildlife managers than in the United States (Alexander 1989, 36).

Little controversy exists over the gamekeepers' role in managing habitat, especially the heather (a wild, low-growing shrub with purple, urn-shaped flowers) essential for grouse. It shelters the birds from weather and predators, and its young shoots make up 90 percent of the adult grouse's diet. One of Adamson's important management tasks, therefore, comes in early spring when he burns patches of land on the estate to promote new heather growth.

In other habitats, gamekeepers manage for red deer—a smaller version of the North American elk. On the 25,000-acre Invermearn Estate in Glen Lyon, Scotland, for example, 500 free-roaming red deer are under the watchful eye of gamekeeper Bob Bissett. Based on an interview with Bissett, Brian Alexander explains that herd improvement is accomplished "by selective culling during the stalking season, which runs from July to October for stags and October to February for hinds. He [Bissett] weeds out the hummels (stags with no antlers), the deformed, and those weakened by age" (Alexander 1989, 40).

American outdoor writer George Reiger experienced this brand of deer hunting and management first-hand and was impressed. In America, Reiger notes, one often hears a hunter brag about long shots at big-game animals. In England, the emphasis is on stalking the quarry to minimize distance, thus assuring a cleaner kill. Says Reiger, the rules

> leave no doubt that a stalker must take his role as an instrument of wildlife management very seriously. One clause in the agreement I signed with Sport of Scotland stated: "Fines may be imposed, depending on the circumstances, *for a wounded animal, a lost animal after being hit, or a miss,* or for spoilt venison due to animals being shot through the haunch or saddle. The penalties will be based on the current wholesale price of venison." (Reiger 1987, 39)

Is red deer hunting only for the elite? Not necessarily. Excluding air travel to England, costs are comparable to what nonresident hunters pay for a week-long elk hunt in the Rocky Mountains. The variety of services is fantastic. John Ormiston, a Scottish hunter and outfitter, says a week of deer stalking typically involves three couples who lease an estate which includes the services of a cook, maid, and gamekeeper for less than $500 per couple. Couples alternate with one another in selecting a daily activity. One day a couple may choose to stalk deer, the next, shoot grouse, the next, fly-fish for Atlantic salmon, and the next, visit castles or tour the local countryside. Compare this with a week elk hunting in Montana, where a couple will spend either $435 each for a nonresident hunting license if they apply through the lottery system and are selected or nearly $1,000 each for a guaranteed hunting license that requires hunting with an outfitter whose services average $1,500 per hunter per week for guide service, food, and lodging. The cost of an elk hunt will be much higher for exclusive hunting privileges (e.g., $9,500 per week on Ted Turner's ranch, see chapter 4) such as those provided in Scotland.

Reiger believes that the British system using gamekeepers provides an ideal environment for long-term stewardship, because the game belongs to landowners "rather than an amorphous proprietor known as the people" (1987, 38).

American guides tend to plan only from year to year, while British keepers generally plan for the decade. Yet only the ownership, meaning the complete control, of the game makes long-term management possible. British keepers actually do what their more thoughtful American counterparts can mostly dream of doing. (Reiger 1987, 39)

Medicinal Magic

Enviro-capitalists are also at work preserving "the slugs and bugs" or, more generally, biodiversity. Tropical rain forests' large inventories of species offer especially fertile ground for pharmaceutical companies interested in the potential medicinal value of wild plants. With the expectation of capturing significant returns, enviro-capitalists have begun to surface with new ideas on linking profits to rain forest preservation.

History is replete with drug discoveries from wild plants. In the 1750s, digitalis, used to treat heart failure, was found in the European foxglove plant. In the 1950s, vincristine sulfate, the drug of choice in the treatment of childhood leukemia, was discovered in the Madagascan periwinkle plant. More recently, taxol, approved for treatment of ovarian cancer, was extracted from the Pacific yew, a small tree growing in the Pacific Northwest forests of the United States.

Nowhere is the likelihood for plant-derived wonder drugs greater than in the world's tropical rain forests. These forests are said to contain more than half the world's estimated 500,000 plant species. Yet fewer than 1 percent have been thoroughly researched for medicinal benefit.

Spurred by both economic and environmental pay-offs, Lisa Conte is one enviro-capitalist who sees green gold in the forests. At just thirty years of age, Conte founded Shaman Pharmaceutical, a biotechnology firm unlike any other listed on the NASDAQ stock exchange. One of the firm's distinctions is its novel approach to drug discovery. Traditional discovery processes rely on the random screening of thousands of plants in the hope of finding a chemical compound with therapeutic value. That process is time-consuming and costly. Instead, Shaman employs a mix of ethnobotany (the study of how native healers use plants), modern medicine, and modern chemistry to find candidates. Ethnobotanists at the firm work with native healers to identify and evaluate the plants they use to treat diseases in their cultures. The active ingredient in the plant then becomes a candidate for further testing and development. Conte and the scientists employed at Shaman believe that this approach can dramatically reduce the costs and improve the odds of discovering important medicines. In addition, by employing indigenous people to record and gather plants, Shaman gives residents more incentive to protect their forests.

Starting Shaman in May 1990 was a courageous move. Lacking any outside funding, Conte charged $40,000 to her credit cards to open Shaman's doors. More seed money soon followed; first $310,000, then $5.8 million, and finally $7.9 million from venture capitalists (Royte 1993, 59). In 1993, Shaman went public with a stock offering that raised another $41 million. The firm attracted capital because investors liked the potential for significantly reducing the time and costs of drug discovery. Also, because Conte's sales talent has attracted the best scientists, the company has cornered the United States market for ethnobotany. The company also has an active scientific advisory board composed of a Nobel Prize winner, a noted professor of chemistry at Columbia University, and a professor emeritus from Harvard University who spent four decades studying the medicinal uses of plants and fungi in the Colombian Amazon basin.

While still a risky venture, Shaman is on a much faster track than the more traditional biotech companies. Its treatment for respiratory viral infections, Provir, entered Phase I clinical safety trials only sixteen months after research began. "No other start-up has moved so quickly from concept to clinical trials" (Royte 1993, 56). The active ingredient, SP-303, isolated from a medicinal plant that grows naturally in Latin America, has been used in local folk medicine for centuries. Shaman is also clinically testing a treatment for genital herpes and developing a medicine for thrush, an oral fungal infection that often afflicts AIDS patients.[6] Both drugs are derived from a plant found in the South American forests.

Shaman uses commercialism to preserve both rain forests and the cultural diversity of forest people. In 1992, the company founded the Healing Forest Conservancy, a not-for-profit organization that promotes the conservation of tropical forests and the welfare of those who live in them. To this end, the company donated 13,333 shares of Shaman's common stock to the conservancy's operating budget. The conservancy's current projects include one called Medicine Woman and another called TerraNova. Medicine Woman is designed to educate and provide technical training for local women in developing countries to inventory plants and work with native healers. TerraNova gives technical and financial support for the establishment and operation of a 3,000-acre ethnobiomedical reserve, deeded to the Traditional Healers Association of Belize (Healing Conservancy n.d., 3–4). In addition, Shaman carries out public project support agreements directly with local communities in exchange for local knowledge. Some 20 percent of its plant-prospecting budget is used to help finance water, school, and other community projects in exchange for local healers' knowledge about medicinal flora (Burton 1994). Shaman intends to funnel some future profits from any discoveries—if they materialize—to projects for the indigenous people who depend on rain forests for their livelihoods.

Part of the allure for Conte and her associates to invest in such a risky business is the potential for huge financial rewards from discovering and marketing the next great wonder drug, but another is the desire to combine the potential profits from a commercial venture in the lucrative drug market with saving rain forests. In true enviro-capitalist form, Lisa Conte believes that the only way to spare rain forests is to increase their economic value, which is precisely what the profits from Shaman are doing.

Minding Our Own Business

Believing that more governmental regulation is necessary to improve the environment, many environmental groups have thwarted potential enviro-capitalism around the world. For example, while the market for African wildlife shows tremendous potential for game management on private and public property, restrictions on wildlife trade discourage entrepreneurship. Under the Convention on International Trade in Endangered Species (CITES), products from endangered species cannot be traded across the borders of parties to the convention. Therefore, though elephant populations thrive in southern Africa to the point of causing serious grazing damage to their habitat, the products of elephants cannot be traded because they are listed as endangered under CITES. South Africa's Kruger National Park has had to cull elephants to keep populations within the carrying capacity of the park. In the past, export of ivory and skins helped pay for culling operations. But with the CITES ban precluding trade, the park is finding it hard to manage elephant herds on its shrinking budgets. In a country where competition for public funds is keen, culling can provide an important alternative funding source as well as being a management tool. In short, CITES stifles environmental entrepreneurship in Kruger National Park.

Offsetting intervention by the international environmental community are innovative institutions that encourage environmental entrepreneurs. Fishing rights in England, hunting rights for wildlife on private lands in South Africa, and contracting for pharmaceutical discoveries in the rain forests of Latin America offer examples of how legal institutions in other countries foster such enterprise. In the United States, enviro-capitalists have faced a greater challenge because federal and state laws make private management of fish and wildlife costly, and public lands limit control of habitat. Even where fee hunting and fishing are used on private land, entrepreneurs have far less flexibility than do Varty and Bernstein with Conscorp in South Africa. Public land management in the United States would make it difficult for Lisa Conte to explore for pharmaceuticals. In at least a few cases, less developed countries are encouraging innovative contracting for environmental assets. In all these cases, the key ingredient is an institutional environment hospitable to private ownership and contracting.

Notes

1. Conversions from rand were made assuming $1 dollar is equal to approximately 3.66 South African rand.

2. One hectare is equivalent to 2.471 acres.

3. All references to terms of agreement between Conscorp and the landowners come from Conscorp's Articles of Association provided to Terry Anderson when he visited the company in 1995.

4. Prices were taken from the *Statistical Abstract of Iceland, 1991* and *1994*.

5. Financial information is from the British Butterfly Conservation Society (N.d.). Conversions from pounds were made assuming £1 is equivalent to approximately $1.50 in U.S. dollars.

6. Data from Shaman Pharmaceutical Shareholder Report dated 18 May 1995.

References

Alexander, Bryan. 1989. Keepers of the Game. *International Wildlife*, September-October.

British Butterfly Conservation Society. N.d. *Butterfly Conservation 1994 Annual Review*. Number 3. Essex, England: British Butterfly Conservation Society Ltd.

Burton, Thomas M. 1994. Drug Company Looks to Witch Doctors to Conjure Products. *Wall Street Journal*, July 7.

Conroy, Andrew. 1992. Wildlife Ranching in South Africa. *Bylae in Landbouweekblad* (Pretoria), October 23.

Doughty, Robin W. 1979. Farming Iceland's Seafowl: The Eider Duck. *Sea Frontiers*, November-December.

Healing Forest Conservancy. N.d. Purpose and Priorities (brochure). Washington, DC: Healing Forest Conservancy.

Hyman, Randall. 1982. Iceland's Harvest of Plenty. *International Wildlife*, May-June.

Kirkland, Paul. N.d. Butterfly Reserves Report. In *Butterfly Conservation 1994 Annual Review*. Number 3. Essex, England: British Butterfly Conservation Society Ltd.

Koch, Eddie. 1995. Hunting for Solutions. *Optima*, August.

Luhsche, Sven. 1995. Conservation That Pays Its Way. *Sunday Times* (Johannesburg, South Africa), September 10.

McDowell, Patrick. 1995. S. Africa Sells Wildlife in Name of Conservation. *Los Angeles Times*, August 20.

Phillips, Andrew. 1992. *Introducing Butterfly Conservation*. Essex, England: British Butterfly Conservation Society Ltd.

Reiger, George. 1987. Public vs. Private Hunting. *Field & Stream*, March.

Ridley, Matt. 1992. Grouse for Better or Worse. *Country Life*, July.

Royte, Elizabeth. 1993. The Shaman and the Scientist. *San Francisco Focus*, August.

Scott, Sue. 1993. Greenland Salmon Fishery Ends. *News Release Communiqué*, August 1. Atlantic Salmon Federation: St. Andrews, New Brunswick, Canada.

Weintraub, Pamela. 1993. Save the Salmon. *ECO*, June.

Chapter 8

Community Spirit

We need to unleash community energy, enabling local people to become stewards of their watersheds and fisheries.

—Les Dominy
Atlantic Salmon Federation

We normally associate entrepreneurship with private, for-profit firms, but it can also be found in community groups and even local governments. For example, members of the Glendive Chamber of Commerce (chapter 1) capitalized on an opportunity to turn waste into wealth at a time when the town's coffers were empty, and local businesses were themselves struggling to survive. These entrepreneurs set their sights on raising revenues from the sale of paddlefish caviar for community projects. This example fits the enviro-capitalist genre because it gets the incentives right; profits accrue to the community shareholders and to the resource itself.

Spurred by entrepreneurial profits, community spirit for amenities is occurring elsewhere. For example, the White Mountain Apache Tribe uses the profits generated from fee hunting for trophy elk to upgrade recreational facilities and start other profitable enterprises on the Fort Apache Reservation in Arizona. In Zimbabwe, innovative conservationists and policy makers are trying to promote wildlife conservation through a program called the Communal Areas Management Programme for Indigenous Resources (CAMPFIRE). The philosophy behind CAMPFIRE is simple: If rural communities can manage and profit from wildlife on their communal lands, they will have a vested interest in sustaining wildlife populations. Similarly, rural communities in Newfoundland and Quebec have taken over the management reins for fee-based recreational fisheries and wildlife areas. In Texas, state park managers have adopted entrepreneurial incentives to boost incomes and lower costs in state parks. Getting the incentives right for community enviro-capitalists can be as important as fostering environmental entrepreneurship in the private sector.

Trophy Elk, Tribal Profits

Night is falling. A pickup truck hauls hunters and guide toward the base camp. A full day of hiking has left the hunters tired but happy. They should be. After five days of hunting, they have harvested five trophy-sized elk. The last one seems headed for the record book. The guide confirms everyone's hopes the next morning when he announces that the latest bull has scored a whopping 404 points. That score easily surpasses the minimum 375 points required for entry into the Boone and Crockett record book. Record elk aside, the hunt has been a once-in-a-lifetime experience for each member of the hunting party. Indeed, no one would blame them for a little boasting. The average score for the five bulls taken on the trip is an incredible 369 Boone and Crockett points, a feat comparable to a five-man bowling team tallying an average score of 275 or a golf foursome shooting two under par.

Given today's crowded hunting conditions, it is hard to imagine that such an experience actually took place in the United States. But it did on the renowned Fort Apache Reservation in east central Arizona managed by the 9,000-member White Mountain Apache Tribe. At 1.6 million acres, this area is as vast as it is wild. The habitat is diverse, from oak chaparral at lower elevations to mixed conifer forests up higher. Most important, it contains what is arguably the highest quality elk herd in North America.

Results over the last twenty years suggest the quality of elk hunting on the reservation. From 1977 to 1995, nontribal hunters have taken ninety bull elk that have made the record books of Boone and Crockett, Safari Club, or Pope and Young. (This is about the same number of record-book elk taken from the state of Montana since record-keeping began in 1932.) The average score for bull elk taken on the reservation during this period stands at 366 Boone and Crockett points, with the highest "typical" bull scoring 404 points and the highest "nontypical" scoring 445 points. As of 1996, the nontypical high scoring bull ranks second worldwide. Since 1980, nontribal hunters have enjoyed a 90 to 95 percent success rate on guided trophy elk hunts.[1] Elk hunting on the reservation has not always been this good. Prior to 1977, hunting was considered decent relative to nearby state and national forest lands but certainly not exceptional. At that time, the Arizona Game and Fish Department managed elk hunting on the reservation, and like most state game agencies, this one emphasized maximizing the number of hunter days rather than the quality of hunting. The numbers reflected the state's approach. Each season, the state would issue 700 nontribal hunting licenses at $150 each. For the period 1970–1976, three record-book elk were harvested on the reservation (Jojola 1989).

Entrepreneurship by the White Mountain Apache Tribe changed the quality of elk hunting dramatically. Under tribal management, the emphasis has been on greatly reducing hunting pressure on immature bulls so they will have a chance to grow to trophy size. As a result, the number of record-book elk harvested has increased from just three over the final six years of state management to an average of eight per season recorded from 1993 through 1995.[2]

As with many entrepreneurial efforts, the tribe had to overcome a significant legal hurdle before it could fully realize its goal of managing for trophy elk. Tribal leaders knew that in order to implement their trophy elk program, they would have to assume complete authority over management of the elk herd and hunting on the reservation. So in 1977, Phillip Stago, director of Fort Apache recreation programs, informed the state that the tribe was assuming complete control of hunting on the reservation. The state responded by removing state game wardens from the reservation during the 1977 hunting season. But from 1977 to 1981, the state continued to require state elk licences for hunting on the reservation and used its authority to arrest several reservation hunters who had not purchased a state licence. The tribe saw this as an infringement on what it believed was its jurisdiction over reservation fish and wildlife resources. In 1977, the tribe filed suit in federal court, asking the court to rule against the state of Arizona's requirement for a state-issued elk tag for hunters on the reservation. In 1981, the court ruled in favor of the Mescalero Apache Tribe in New Mexico in a similar suit, thereby setting a precedent for all tribes. As a result, the White Mountain Apache now have clear legal jurisdiction over reservation fish and wildlife and activities related to them.[3]

While the lawsuit was pending, the tribe began to work on its trophy elk program. In 1977, its first year of operation, the tribe issued twelve trophy elk permits at $750 each, compared to the state issue of 700 nontribal permits at $150. With that one move, the tribe had dramatically reduced elk hunting pressure. In 1979, the tribe hired its first full-time biologist, John Cade, and raised the number of trophy elk permits to thirty-two, at $1,500 each.

Since its 1977 inception, revenues from the program have continued to grow. In 1995, for example, they totaled over $850,000. Sixty-six hunters paid $12,000 each for a seven-day trophy hunt. In addition, a special auction for four additional hunts was also held, with an average winning bid of $24,000 and a high bid of $30,000.[4] The $12,000 price tag is obviously high, but as tribal leaders correctly perceived, a growing number of hunters are willing to pay a premium to enjoy the elk hunting experience available on Fort Apache.

To protect its investment in trophy elk, the tribe made concessions in the operation of its other enterprises on the reservation. For example, tribal attorney Robert Brauchli points out that livestock grazing has been drastically reduced to provide more forage for elk. Even the tribe's lucrative timber program has changed. Tribal biologists review every timber sale to minimize impact on elk. As a general rule, notes Joseph Jojola, no logging is allowed in high country areas, riparian zones, and mountain meadows. In areas where logging is allowed, it is timed to avoid critical elk calving periods, and roads are closed after logging is finished to minimize disruption of elk habitat.

The reservation also offers less expensive hunting opportunities. For example, to maintain proper bull-to-cow ratio in the herd, the tribe periodically issues cow permits at $300 each. Hunters' success rate is 80 percent. Other hunting opportunities include a $150 permit to hunt bear, a $75 permit to hunt javelina, and a $75 permit to hunt wild turkey. For $50 per season or $5 per day hunters can hunt quail, tree squirrels, and cottontail rabbits.

In addition to hunting, the Fort Apache Reservation offers many other recreational opportunities that the tribe regulates and charges for. Fishing is restricted to flies and lures in some areas, and species include native Apache trout (catch and release only), arctic grayling, bass, and northern pike. Yearly fishing permits cost $80, summer permits $50, and daily permits $5. There is even a rent-a-lake program available on Cyclone Lake that gives exclusive use of the lake for $300 per day. Like hunting, fishing has proven lucrative, generating over $600,000 in 1995. The reservation also offers camping, boating, and river rafting. In the future the tribe hopes to initiate photographic safaris.

Fee-based recreation has had a positive impact on the reservation's economy. In 1995, the tribe's game and fish department reported that recreation generated nearly $2 million in revenues. These monies were spent on habitat enhancements, recreational facility improvements, and seed money for business start-ups on the reservation. Beyond revenues, the hunting and recreation programs have generated jobs for hunting guides, outfitters, cooks, and field researchers.

Gather Around the CAMPFIRE

Darkness comes quickly to the East Caprivi, being so close to the Equator. Bevan Munyali, a village game scout, appointed by his community who live in this region of Namibia, helps light the fires.

Together with the other men, they will spend the night in this farmer's corn field, trying to protect their food crops from the elephants. Usually it is the lone bulls that come, as they have each night this week, trampling the crops and eating hundreds of pounds of corn as they pass through the area. Bevan is worried. He must balance the farmer's concerns regarding the elephant with his own task, which is to help his community to conserve their natural resources and the wildlife in the area.

Hours slip past. Bevan and the farmer doze beside the glowing embers. But then the crack of dry branches wakes them, indicating that something big is moving in their direction. Two fully grown bull elephants crash into the field. The farmer shouts to wake the others, and in unison they start banging steel pots together. The elephants turn to face the noise, their sensitive ears flapping in aggravation. Then they charge. Three tons of muscle standing eighteen feet high at the shoulder, the bulls rush forward, sending the farmer and his family running for safety.

Realizing the danger, Bevan fires two blasts from his shotgun into the air, in the hope that the elephants retreat. Instead, one of the bulls wheels around and heads straight towards him. Defenseless, Bevan retreats from the field. The elephants continue on their way, eating and trampling the ripe corn underfoot. No doubt, the farmer and his family will be short of food for the remainder of the year. (Hylton n.d., 5)

This account of a peasant farmer's struggle against wild animals is rarely portrayed in Hollywood versions of African wildlife, but it is a situation that Victoria Hylton of Africa Resources Trust often sees. She and her colleagues in the conservation movement in southern Africa realize that idyllic scenes of wild animals freely roaming vast savannahs are rapidly vanishing from the landscape because those animals too often compete with the humans struggling for survival on the same turf. Although southern African nations have set aside 18 percent of the land as national parks and wildlife preserves, human population pressure is reducing wildlife habitat and poaching is reducing wildlife herds.

Hylton and her counterparts understand that the wildlife management problems result because indigenous people trying to live off the land must compete with wildlife; hence, wildlife is a liability rather than an asset. These people generally resent the fact that land is being set aside for animals rather than for people. Moreover, out of the parks and reserves come lions, leopards, elephants, and hippopotamuses that range onto communal lands where they destroy crops and livestock and occasionally people.

Entrepreneurs who understand the problems of wildlife management in southern Africa are working with local communities and national governments to change the incentives faced by indigenous people on their communal lands. Between 60 and 80 percent of Africa's people live in rural areas, and the overwhelming majority of them barely scrape by with subsistence farming and ranching. The lands they use are communally owned, and the soils are often poor for growing crops or forage for cattle. These same lands that are marginal for agriculture, however, can provide excellent wildlife habitat. The problem is that sustainable wildlife populations have not meant sustainable human populations.

With research and support from the Center for Applied Social Sciences of the University of Zimbabwe, the Ford Foundation, and the World Wildlife Fund, Zimbabwe's government is trying to change this through the innovative Communal Areas Management Programme for Indigenous Resources (CAMPFIRE). CAMPFIRE is an "entrepreneurial approach to rural development" (Environmental Consultants 1990, 3) based on the principle that the benefits from wildlife must go to those who pay the financial and social costs of coexisting with wild animals. The CAMPFIRE concept devolves the responsibility of managing wildlife to local communities that can profit from it.

The Nyaminyami District Council, with a human population of 35,000 and communal lands totaling 363,000 hectares, offers a prime example of how CAMPFIRE can work. In 1989, its inaugural year, Nyaminyami's CAMPFIRE project generated $108,800[5] from safari hunting and another $18,800 from culling to keep local wildlife populations under control. With the major capital costs of $80,773 covered by funds donated by conservation groups, the district had $6,400 to distribute among the twelve separate communities after paying operating and administrative costs and allocating 12 percent for capital investment and reserves (Thresher 1993, 45). If these amounts seem small, realize that the average cash income per household was less than $100 per year in 1989.

Another early CAMPFIRE success came in the Beitbridge District. However, unlike Nyaminyami, the Beitbridge project was financed completely by the returns from wildlife. Recognizing that different communities within the district make more sacrifices to provide wild-life habitat, the Beitbridge Council distributed wildlife profits un-equally to communities within the district, giving more to those communities that produced more, higher-value animals. In 1990, the Beitbridge District CAMPFIRE project generated approximately $20,000 from hunting. Of that amount, the community of Chikwara-kwara received 87 percent of the total, because it was the top wildlife producer. Two other neighboring communities received much smaller amounts because of lower animal numbers. National parks also paid the Beitbridge District Council $18,400 for revenues accrued from past safari hunting, and from this amount, Chikwarakwara received an-other $8,000. Free to determine how to use their proceeds, the people of Chikwarakwara decided to pay each of the 149 households in the community $80 as a wildlife dividend. The remainder of the earnings went toward building a school and purchasing a corn-grinding mill. Though the $80 dividend may not seem like a lot to wealthy western-ers, it almost doubled the average annual cash income for each family.

Attitudes toward wildlife are changing among the people involved with CAMPFIRE. "Now the people of Beitbridge are reported to be talking seriously about how to control poaching. They are considering the possibility of reducing a household's cash payment by the value of any animal poached by any of its members, e.g., Z$75 for an impala" (Thresher 1993, 50).

CAMPFIRE projects in other districts have taken their cue from these early successes. The Binga District project capitalizes on its long shore-line at the western end of Lake Kariba and the adjacent Chizaria Na-tional Park, which forms a repository for wildlife roaming onto communal lands. The project includes a lease with a private hunting safari operator and joint ventures with two photographic safari opera-tors. Plans are also under way for a commercial fishing venture. The Hwange District is developing the "scenic attractions and natural re-sources" near the Zambezi River and Victoria Falls by forming joint ventures with two photographic safari operators who are building tourist camps in the areas (Environmental Consultants 1990, 23). Bula-lima Mangwe District has set aside a marshy area west of the Natal River for an elephant herd that forms the basis for safari hunting agree-ments between the district council and private operators.

Communities carrying out CAMPFIRE projects have adopted a vari-ety of ways to use their wildlife, depending on local environmental and economic factors. Controlled safari hunting is currently the use of wildlife with the highest value, but other revenue sources include wildlife-based tourism and natural products such as hides, meat, crocodile eggs, and wood, harvested on a sustainable basis.

Though most projects are in their infancy, strong signs are already evident that poaching and habitat loss wanes when the wildlife becomes an asset to the local people. How effectively these programs will promote wildlife conservation in the future depends on whether the local communities bearing the brunt of wildlife costs are allowed to continue benefiting directly from their management efforts. Some evidence suggests that bureaucrats in the central government are beginning to skim off some of the profits, and if this continues, the success of CAMPFIRE may be short-lived.

Spawning for Dollars

After years of reducing river pollution and temporarily halting the netting of Atlantic salmon on the high seas, Les Dominy of the Atlantic Salmon Federation believes it will be local Canadian communities and sportsmen who will supply the final piece of the recovery puzzle. In Dominy's view, because "governments are simply running out of money," it is necessary "to unleash community energy, enabling local people to become stewards of their watersheds and fisheries" (quoted in Robinson 1994, 22). Moreover, by devolving authority, locals who tend to resist top-down regulations can use local knowledge to take account of the idiosyncracies of each salmon river. As with other examples of enviro-capitalists, local responsibility along with the right economic incentives can foster strong local stewardship. According to the Atlantic Salmon Federation's Dr. John Anderson, "When communities and sportsmen have a vested interest in their local river, they begin to think of it as 'ours'; they want to do what they can to take care of it and increase production" (quoted in Robinson 1994, 22).

The Exploits River near Grand Falls, Newfoundland, provides an excellent example of what can happen with community management of an Atlantic salmon fishery. Initially using public funding, the community constructed a fish elevator that allows salmon to climb past the 150-foot waterfall on the river. In the past, the waterfall prevented fish from migrating any further than nine miles upstream for spawning. But construction of the fishway opened 200 additional miles of river for salmon spawning. The increase in salmon production is astounding. Prior to the opening of the fish elevator in 1989, the Exploits River had a maximum of only 2,000 spawning salmon, and that was under ideal conditions. But only four years after the elevator became fully operational, spawning salmon numbered 20,000. Looking down the road, the prospects are even brighter, as local managers anticipate 100,000 returning fish in the next six years (Robinson 1994, 24).

The fish elevator project was spearheaded by Environment Resources Management Association (ERMA), a community, nonprofit private organization. Conceived in 1983 and operational in 1985, the organization is an offshoot of early efforts by the Grand Falls Chamber of Commerce to enhance salmon fishing prospects on the Exploits River and thus bring the community more sportsmen's dollars. To launch its elevator project, ERMA submitted a proposal to various government agencies for financial support. Funded with dollars from the national government, ERMA employs fifty people to operate the elevator, as well as an ultramodern hatchery and interpretation center.

The economic impact in the community is being felt as the increase in salmon has attracted more fishermen to the community. ERMA manager Fred Parsons says he remembers when the number of fishermen on the Exploits numbered only 1,500 per season. Now ten times that number flock to the river.[6] According to Parsons, the Exploits River even competes effectively with salmon fishing on the Gander River, a world-famous salmon fishery in central Newfoundland. Parsons estimates, conservatively, that the Exploits salmon fishery is bringing in roughly $2 million to the community. The interpretation center brings additional dollars from the 40,000 visitors per year.[7]

Because sport salmon fishing is so important to the community's economy, ERMA has its own all-volunteer, antipoaching patrol. Capitalizing on the immense popularity of the river among local fishermen, ERMA trains them to spot poaching activities. Volunteers are provided with a crest and a cap to let other fishermen know that the river is under constant surveillance.

While public funding launched this community effort, Parsons and fellow ERMA members are working to establish a fee fishing system to fund the organization's operating costs for the fishway, the hatchery, the interpretation center, and future projects. "This will be tricky at first," says Parsons, because local fishermen want their turf for fishing and fear that big dollars from visiting fishermen will push them off the river. But Parsons believes that a well-planned fee fishing program can relieve these anxieties. For example, ERMA is entertaining the idea of creating different fishing sections along the river to provide more options for fishermen. Some sections will be more exclusive and therefore command higher fees. Other sections will be open to all at lower fees.

A realist, Parsons thinks that the government gas tank is nearly empty and therefore private conservationists and communities must devise and support efforts to produce natural amenities. In Parsons's words, "The day of barking at the government is long gone. We want to be part of the solution."[8]

Next door, in the province of Quebec, cooperation among eclectic local groups has become an integral part of the community solution for another salmon river. The provincial government tried for years to limit salmon gill-netting by the Micmac Indians at the mouth of the Cascapedia River, but to no avail. Then, in 1992, they tried a different tack. The government agreed to allow a local board to take over management of the fishery and let this be financed by Cascapedia user fees. The composition of the board lent itself to cooperation from the start because half of the board members were Micmac Indians while the other half were local sportsmen and other community members.

In two years, a new spirit of cooperation took hold at the Cascapedia River salmon fishery. Gill-netting was greatly reduced by the Micmacs, and in return, Micmacs were trained as river guides and river guardians. Today, more than 100 Micmacs are employed as guides and private wardens and in other activities related to the salmon sport fishery on the Cascapedia River. The incomes they earn and the revenues generated for the tribe and the local economy from fishing fees more than compensate for the reduced gill-netting. Salmon caught commercially were worth about $30 but their worth rises $400 when caught by a sport fisher (Robinson 1994, 25). Harmony, conservation, and a lucrative sport fishery are the by-products of local community management.

Comfort Zones

The Cascapedia River story is not the only community solution in Quebec largely because of the provincial government's establishment of ZECs (Zones d'Exploitation Contrôlées). A ZEC is an area of Crown land (land owned by the province) where fishing and hunting rights, as well as access rights, are managed by a local group for the benefit of the public. On these lands, the public pays various fees to the local management group to hunt and fish. The proceeds go to paying for the management of the ZEC. Currently, Quebec has eighty-two such zones covering approximately 11.6 million acres of Crown lands (Ministère de l'Environnement et de la Faune 1995).

According to Yannick Routhier of the Ministère de l'Environnement et de la Faune, the ZEC system was the provincial government's response to social and economic change. For nearly a century, starting in the 1880s, the government leased much of its best hunting and fishing areas to private clubs. It was an arrangement that was generally welcomed by the public, although game poaching by locals was a constant problem. Leasing to clubs was a source of revenue to the provincial government, and the clubs were the protectors of the resource for which they were paying. In addition, the clubs, often situated in remote areas of the province, hired substantial numbers of local people as club managers, guides, wardens, cooks, maids, and maintenance workers. After World War II, public acceptance began to wane as the province became industrialized. More people had more money and leisure time for recreation and in turn demanded more Crown lands be opened up to them. Between 1965 and 1978, the government responded by canceling about half the area leases to private clubs and turning the areas into Crown-managed reserves available to all for recreation. As more land entered the reserve system, government expenses became prohibitive. By the end of the 1970s, the government decided against the creation of new reserves and began establishing ZECs.

In 1978, the government established the first of many hunting and fishing ZECs in the province. Hunting and fishing ZECs include hunting for such species as bear, moose, and deer and fishing for such species as walleye and trout. Two years later, the government established several Atlantic salmon river ZECs to capitalize on the growing popularity of inland sport salmon fishing. Each salmon ZEC provides access to rivers that have Atlantic salmon runs, as well as anadromous brook char and landlocked brook char. In 1987, the government expanded the use of ZECs to include a waterfowl ZEC.

Each ZEC is a nonprofit corporation with a board of directors that contracts with the government to develop recreation through user fees, to assist in monitoring fish and wildlife populations, and to set and enforce seasonal harvest regulations in conjunction with government guidelines. Initially, the national government provided start-up costs for ZECs and even covered some operating costs where user fees were insufficient. As of 1995, however, all ZECs were required to rely on their own income for support.

According Yannick Routhier, the management concept for ZECs is best characterized as a kind of co-op whereby users, through their elected representatives on the managing board of directors, have a voice in managing recreational use and controlling wildlife resources.[9]

Routhier notes that many ZEC boards have broadened their composition to include other local interests, such as chambers of commerce and local tribes that want to promote economic opportunities from ZEC amenities. For example, the Corporation de resturation de la Jacques-Cartier has responsibility for managing the Rivière-Jacques-Cartier, an Atlantic salmon sport fishery located approximately 100 miles northeast of Quebec City. Its board of directors is composed of eighteen members, nine of whom are elected by recreational users and nine of whom come from municipalities within the river basin. The Rivière-Des-Escoumins, another salmon fishery located 150 miles northeast of Quebec City, has a board composed of one-third recreational users, one-third local municipalities, and one-third Montagnais Indians (Ministère de l'Environnement et de la Faune 1994, 7).

Unlike the national forests in the United States, where hunting and fishing access and road use are free, the Canadian organizations charge fees for nearly every activity. ZEC memberships cost about $15, and road use fees are $4.00 per day or $30 per year. Fees for hunting and fishing vary. The average daily fishing fee for species other than Atlantic salmon ranges from $8.75 to $11. The daily rate for fishing in a salmon ZEC, the *crème de la crème* of sport fishing, runs as high as $55. Fees also vary with exclusivity of use. On the Ste-Marguerite salmon ZEC, for example, a ZEC member pays a daily salmon fishing fee of $23 on sections where rods are unlimited compared with $43 in a limited-rod section. Nonmembers enjoy the same access privileges but at slightly higher user fees. Gross income from fees on the Ste-Marguerite was about $100,000 in 1994, about equal to expenses for maintaining roads, providing private wardens, monitoring wildlife numbers, and carrying out conservation projects. In addition to fee revenues, a well-run ZEC also brings income to local economies. For example, Nelson Bryant (1989) notes in the *New York Times* that salmon fishing on the Ste-Marguerite salmon ZEC resulted in $1.5 million income to the local area.

In addition to steady financial progress, ZECs are improving wildlife management. Jean-François Davignon of the Atlantic Salmon Federation notes widespread improvements in protecting, monitoring, and conserving salmon fisheries (Davignon n.d.). Overall, he points out, ZEC management corporations hire a combined force of 116 auxiliary wardens from local communities to assist the government in protecting wildlife and fisheries. For salmon rivers on the Gaspé peninsula, the numbers of salmon returning to spawn each year are now approaching numbers that will ensure stable river populations down the road under local management. For example, "In 1984, Gaspé peninsula rivers were only at 30 percent of required salmon spawners. Today, they are averaging between 80 percent and 100 percent" (Davignon n.d., 2). As with White Mountain Apache elk management, both the community economies and the wildlife are better off in the hands of enviro-capitalists.

Lone Star Parks

Entrepreneurship is definitely switched on in Texas state parks, such as Big Bend Ranch State Park, one of the largest in the country, with 265,000 acres. One day, park ranger George Menzies III got the idea of allowing park visitors to participate in the spring and fall cattle drives to move the park's 100 longhorn cattle from pasture to pasture. As an entrepreneur, Menzies, of course, saw a profit in the idea. Hence, Big Bend's three-day Longhorn Cattle Drive was born. For $350 and one's own horse and tack (or $450 if the park provides horse and tack), city slickers can hit the trail alongside park staffers and play Rowdy Yates for three days. Activities include rounding up cattle, branding and vaccinating calves, and enjoying chuck wagon meals on the open range.

Entrepreneurship does not end with cattle drives at Big Bend. Adventuresome backpackers may use the thirty miles of hiking trails in the Chihuahua Desert wilderness, available for $6 per hiker per day. For serious students of nature, interpretative bus tours cover park flora and fauna for $60 per person. For low-budget travelers, self-guided tours of the nearby Barton Warnock Environmental Education Center hardly put a dent in the pocketbook at $2.50 for an adult and $1.50 for a child.

Other Texas state parks exhibit their own brand of entrepreneurship. At Big Spring State Park, thousands of sandhill cranes were the inspiration for the annual "Cranefest," a birdwatcher's delight. Park manager Ron Alton, one of the creators of Cranefest, says the gala event includes a $5 luncheon banquet, a $10 dinner banquet, and one-hour demonstrations for $5 on how to rehabilitate injured birds. Bird lovers who fancy the nightlife can kick up their heels on a two-hour nocturnal owl prowl at Brazos Bend State Park for a fee of $5.

These are just a few of the moneymaking strategies park staffers-turned-entrepreneurs have implemented in recent years. All come under a broad new initiative started by the Texas Parks and Wildlife Department, the agency responsible for park management, to make the state park system self-sufficient. "Our goal is 100 percent—to finance all of our [state park] operations out of revenues we raise," says department director Andrew Sampson (quoted in Tomaso 1995). A former director of the Texas Nature Conservancy, Sampson became director of the Parks and Wildlife Department in 1990, a year when appropriations to parks from state general funds totaled $15 million. But a state legislature committed to reducing spending cut park funding in half in 1992, and in 1993, the legislature voted to eliminate general support entirely for 1994 and beyond.

Ron Holliday, head of the department's public lands division, describes the predicament state parks were facing during the summer of 1992: "Declining funding forced the division to propose closures of several parks and reductions in force (RIFs) throughout the state. This announcement drove home the fact that the Texas park system must develop a program of fiscal responsibility just to survive" (Holliday 1995, 24).

Meanwhile, demands on the parks were intensifying. Visitor numbers had risen every year since 1988. In the early 1990s, more than 25 million people visited the half-million-acre state park system—a system that comprises eighty-two state parks, thirty-two historical parks, thirteen partnership parks, and seven natural areas scattered throughout Texas. Compare this with Yellowstone National Park's 2.2 million acres and 3 million visitors per year.

The first step taken to avert park closures was the "partners in parks" program designed to enlist the support of local communities. The communities responded with funding and volunteer work. These efforts kept parks afloat in fiscal year 1993, but trouble still lay ahead for 1994, the year general appropriations were to be eliminated entirely.

In anticipation, Holliday asked his staff to develop an aggressive strategy for keeping parks operational. The strategy they devised led to a program bureaucrats now refer to as the "entrepreneurial budget system" or EBS. In essence, EBS is designed to devolve more of the park management responsibility to park superintendents, while motivating them to produce real cost savings and boost revenue. The motivation for superintendents to increase revenue is that they get to keep as much as 35 percent of whatever additional income they generate for the year and spend it as they see fit on the park the following year. Of the remainder, 40 percent is used as a safety net for areas that are unable to draw many visitors but are considered important to the park system. The other 25 percent is earmarked for a special account to start future EBS programs. All of the budgetary savings realized for the year are kept within the park to enhance the next year's budget. Before EBS, a superintendent was essentially penalized for saving money, since a park's budget for the next year was reduced by the amount saved. "Meanwhile, attempts to increase revenue were rarely acknowledged much less rewarded," Holliday says. "Parks that collected increased revenues often saw those revenues transferred to other parks that made no effort to increase their receipts" (Holliday 1995, 25).

The heart of the program, according to Holliday, is the signed performance agreement, or contract, if you will, between the director of the Texas Parks and Wildlife Department and each park superintendent (Holliday 1995, 25). The agreement specifies the coming year's revenue target, which is the prior year's budget adjusted upward by a growth factor of 0.5 to 3 percent. The agreement states that if park income exceeds that target, the superintendent can keep as much as 35 percent of the excess for spending on the park the following year. After the initial year, Holliday says that "'Doubting Thomases' were won over when oversize checks were presented to 40 of the 42 pilot EBS parks totaling $378,000 at the annual Public Lands Division meeting held in the fall of 1994" (Holliday 1995, 28).

Another key element of EBS is that state park superintendents are given broad latitude in thinking up their own moneymaking strategies provided they meet the first requirement of protecting and preserving park natural resources. Ron Holliday notes that park managers are very careful not to employ a "rubber snake" mentality, referring to activities or products that would cheapen the image of the park.

Of course, balancing park amenities and generating income is always difficult, but director Sampson says park managers have been careful not to exploit the parks' natural and historical values for the sake of profits. After all, these resources are what bring people to the parks in the first place. At Varner-Hogg Historical Park, where wedding receptions are held every other week at $150 to $250 a day, superintendent Fred Hutchinsons points out, "We could easily double that, but I'm concerned about the effects that would have on the grounds" (quoted in Tomaso 1995). Meanwhile, Varner-Hogg's wedding receptions, along with souvenir sales, pay for about half of the operating budget at the site.

In addition to the EBS program, other innovations have improved customer service and thus the bottom line for Texas state parks. For example, the park system's 7,300 campsites formerly had very low camping fees. Now superintendents can charge more for campsites in high demand areas and less for campsites in low demand. At Huntsville State Park, basic campsites are $9, sites with electricity, $12, and sites with screen shelters, $18. These prices are $5 to $9 more than they were previously.

A new centralized reservation system for overnight stays in parks has increased reservations and income by 30 percent after a year of operation. It also makes life easier for the customer and allocates demand more effectively. John Weaver, the official who set up the system, says that in the past

> You had to figure out what park you wanted to go to. You had to find out the phone number, call them, and make your reservation. And if they didn't have anything, you had to start all over again with another park. Now, customers call a single number—(512) 389-8900—to book into any of the eighty-two state parks that allow overnight stays. (quoted in Tomaso 1995)

With the centralized system, callers can get a list of alternative sites if their first choice is taken. Weaver notes that the system also helps steer people to parks that have been underutilized in the past.

Such innovative efforts are bringing Texas state parks through tumultuous changes in funding. When appropriations from general funds were eliminated in 1994, park revenues from user fees totaled $21 million, an increase of more than 33 percent since 1991. The revenue generated in 1994 covered approximately 80 percent of the operating costs, compared to 50 percent in the three prior years. (Dedicated funds from sales taxes on sporting equipment now make up the difference between revenues from user fees and expenditures.)

Moreover, the number of parks turning a profit is growing. In 1993, nine state parks generated a combined total of $802,000 of revenue in excess of spending. A year later, the first year of program implementation, fifteen state parks generated a total of $1.5 million in excess of spending (Tomaso 1995). In 1995, twenty-two parks were in the black. Texas parks' successes have drawn nationwide attention. Says Ney Landrum, executive director of the National Association of State Park Directors, "No other park system has done as much in terms of entrepreneurial financing methods" (quoted in Tomaso 1995).

Working in Strange Places

Community examples of environmental entrepreneurship differ in that they provide collective rather than personal gain. Entrepreneurship at the community level still requires access to amenity markets, the freedom to contract, and well-defined property rights to natural resources. If certain conditions are present, environmental entrepreneurship is even possible in the public sector. A public manager's incentive must be changed from capturing funds at the public trough to raising revenues from the environmental marketplace. Public managers also must be given the same access to amenity markets as private entrepreneurs have; they must be able to charge fees and restrict access. Finally, they must face a bottom line that reflects the difference between revenues collected and operating expenses. When revenues are increased and/or costs are cut, the entrepreneurs must be able to reinvest the profit back into the resource. If these conditions can be created, enviro-capitalists can be as productive in the public sector as they are in the private sector.

Notes

1. Telephone interview with John Cade, assistant director of Game and Fish Department, White Mountain Apache Tribe, 30 January 1996.
2. Telephone interview with John Cade, 30 January 1996.
3. Details on the lawsuit were provided by Robert Brauchli, attorney for the White Mountain Apache Tribe.
4. Telephone interview with John Cade, 30 January 1996.
5. Conversions from Zimbabwean dollars were made assuming Z$1 is equivalent to approximately $0.40 in U.S. dollars.
6. Telephone interview with Fred Parsons, 20 December 1995.
7. Conversions from Canadian dollars were made assuming Can$1 is equivalent to approximately $0.73 in U.S. dollars.
8. Telephone interview with Fred Parsons, 20 December 1995.
9. Telephone interview with Yannick Routhier, 14 September 1995.

References

Bryant, Nelson. 1989. Quebec Zones Aid Fish and Anglers. *New York Times*, July 24.
Davignon, Jean-François. N.d. The Quebec ZEC Story. Atlantic Salmon Federation, Quebec, Canada.
Environmental Consultants (Pvt) Ltd. 1990. *People, Wildlife and Natural Resources—The CAMPFIRE Approach to Rural Development in Zimbabwe*. Harare, Zimbabwe: Zimbabwe Trust.

Holliday, Ron. 1995. Texas' Entrepreneurial Budget System. *Different Drummer*, summer, 24–28.

Hylton, Victoria. N.d. The Wild Harvest. Southern Wild Productions, Johannesburg, South Africa.

Jojola, Joseph R.1989. Fort Apache Elk: White Mountain Apaches Seek to Produce New World Record. *Wapiti*, October.

Ministère de l'Environnement et de la Faune. 1994. Controlled Zones (ZECs): Nature and Operation. Quebec, Canada: Gouvernement du Quebec.

———. 1995. Zones d'Exploitation Contrôlées Statistiques (1990–1995). Quebec, Canada: Gouvernement du Quebec.

Robinson, Jerome B. 1994. The Next Step for Atlantic Salmon. *Field & Stream*, September.

Thresher, Valerie. 1993. Economic Reflections on Wildlife Utilization in Zimbabwe. Masters thesis, University of California at Davis.

Tomaso, Bruce. 1995. Pay as You Play. *Dallas Morning News* (Sunday ed.), July 23.

Chapter 9

The Good, the Bad, and the Ugly

It's unfortunate that we're at the point where the visitor experience
could be affected by this closure [Norris Campground].

—Michael Finley
Yellowstone Park Superintendent

The examples examined in this book show how economic and environmental incentives can motivate environmental entrepreneurs to seek
innovative ways of managing and conserving natural resources. Given
the increasing value of environmental amenities resulting from rising
incomes, the potential is growing for entrepreneurs to capitalize on
opportunities. These opportunities do not necessarily mean that enviro-capitalists can or will solve all environmental problems. As in any
market, the growing demand for environmental amenities means that
people are willing to pay more for the good. Whether entrepreneurs
respond depends on multiple factors, not the least of which is the political and legal environment. The examples offered in the preceding
chapters suggest that when this setting encourages entrepreneurship,
private solutions are an important tool not to be overlooked in establishing environmental policy. When market demands are there to
switch on entrepreneurship, enviro-capitalists have an incentive to respond.

Unfortunately, these incentives do not always exist—especially in
the political sector, as evidenced by the response of Mike Finley, Yellowstone National Park superintendent, to a budget shortfall. In the
spring of 1996, Finley announced the closure of a popular campground
and related facilities because the park's operating costs were outstrip-
ping congressional appropriations by $2 million (Milstein 1996). He
blamed the difference on a "budget cut," meaning that the authorized
budget was less than requested even though it was 10 percent more

167

than the previous year. In Finley's view, park management needed to spend less on customers to avoid a budget shortfall. The usual recourse is to go to Congress and request additional funding. But in an era of deficits, this course is becoming less and less reliable. In the meantime, our national parks are experiencing budget shortfalls and deteriorating customer services.

A logical alternative to closing facilities is to raise money directly from park users, as enviro-capitalists are doing in the Texas state park system. Nearly 3 million people visit Yellowstone annually, and a charge of $7 per visitor would have avoided the 1996 fiscal crisis. Unfortunately, park managers have little incentive to be entrepreneurial in finding new sources of revenue from park users. This point was made in the winter of 1989 when Yellowstone was experiencing another budget shortfall. When asked whether improvements in fee collection would raise park revenues, Bob Barbee, the park's former superintendent, said that spending another $50,000 on fee collection at Yellowstone's gates even at existing rates could generate another $500,000. "You don't have to have a Ph.D. in economics or accounting to understand that this is a good investment," said Barbee. But he wasn't willing to make the investment because the money at the time would go to the federal treasury. He and the park were better off spending Yellowstone's limited budget on catching speeding drivers or preventing ignorant tourists from being gored by bison. In response to the question of why some entrepreneurial congressman didn't propose a change in the system, the superintendent said that it was unlikely that a congressman would support such a proposal because it would reduce congressional power that exists by virtue of controlling the purse strings.[1]

This final chapter examines three cases of political institutions that range from the good—a case where the political and legal institutions encourage entrepreneurial solutions—to the bad—a case where perverse incentives created by restrictions on market alternatives discourage good stewardship—to the ugly—a case where perverse incentives actually destroyed amenities. Our purpose in examining these cases is not to end on a negative note that disparages all political efforts to promote environmental ends. Rather, it is to suggest where legal institutions that unnecessarily raise transaction costs need to be changed so that environmental entrepreneurship can be part of the solution in the political sector, too.

The Good

In 1992, Montana's Department of State Lands announced that it was going to harvest about one million board feet of timber from two state parcels on Mount Ellis near Bozeman. Residents of Eagle Rock Reserve (chapter 6) were not happy with this announcement because Mount Ellis is one of the amenities enjoyed by owners of the lots at Eagle Rock. They believed logging would leave an ugly scar on the side of the mountain similar to those left by logging on national forest lands.

Because state land managers have different incentives than national forest managers,[2] the state gave the Eagle Rock residents the opportunity to purchase a perpetual "viewshed easement" for the land. Unlike national forests, state lands are required to generate income from logging and other activities for the public school trust fund. Hence, the state took the position that if residents at Eagle Rock did not want logging on Mount Ellis, they would have to compensate the public school trust fund for the forgone timber revenues. The price of the easement would be $430,000, the present value of the lost timber revenues.

Residents considered purchasing the easement, but Kurt Tesmer, the state timber sale designer, gave them a cheaper option. Cut from the enviro-capitalist mold, Tesmer saw a way of satisfying both the concerns of Eagle Rock residents and the state's requirement to generate income. He proposed a timber sale that would look much different from the typical clear-cut on national forests. Tesmer said that the state's harvest would mimic the natural openings on Mount Ellis. The sale would leave large, irregular clumps of fir trees standing on the state parcel. The small areas to be harvested would have irregular edges. Believing that Tesmer could deliver cuts that looked natural, residents of Eagle Rock withdrew their opposition and avoided paying the $430,000.

Tesmer's plan worked. Rich Morris, resident manager of Eagle Rock, says, "For the most part, they [Tesmer and the state] succeeded. Next to not taking the logs at all, we got the next-best thing. They succeeded in doing something that it is not noticeably going to change our landscape" (quoted in McMillion 1992). And despite the additional cost of designing and implementing the sensitive harvest, the state sacrificed little in either timber output or profit. Tesmer says, "It most definitely was designed from a standpoint of making it an acceptable visual project. But I don't think we sacrificed a stick of lumber from our original proposal" (quoted in McMillion 1992). In generating $100,000 for schools at a cost of $50,000 and producing a visually attractive harvest, Kurt Tesmer's Mount Ellis timber sale illustrates what can happen when the incentives are right for an enviro-capitalist in the political sector.

Unfortunately, on nearby national forest lands little, if any, incentive exists for enviro-capitalism. The reason is simple. Because state foresters are required to generate profits for public schools, they are forced to consider all revenue-generating potential, including timber and amenity values. The U.S. Forest Service, on the other hand, has no such connection between revenue and costs. Most revenues from timber sales go the treasury, while operating funds come from congressional appropriations. Without a link between revenues and costs, officials have little incentive to search for creative ways to generate income from environmentally sensitive logging. Economic performance reflects these different incentives. Over the 1988–1992 period, Montana state lands averaged $2 in revenue for every dollar spent selling timber, while the Forest Service averaged only $0.50 (Leal 1995). Thus, the state generated nearly $14 million in income from timber sales, while the Forest Service lost $42 million. Remarkably, the state harvested only one-twelfth the volume harvested by the Forest Service. Moreover, based on a 1992 independent environmental audit, state foresters actually scored higher than federal foresters in protecting watersheds from logging impacts (Leal 1995, 11). State management also resulted in higher quality timber reserves (Leal 1995, 12–13).

As with Texas state parks (chapter 8), entrepreneurship can be fostered in the political sector. Forced by the state legislature to move toward self-support, Texas park personnel have come up with a host of revenue-raising services for customers that have led to a 67 percent increase in revenue collected from park visitors. A growing number of state parks are following the Texas lead. Custer State Park in South Dakota, for example, generates revenues from a variety of services, including a "Buffalo Safari jeep ride" to the interior of the park, a walk-in-only fishing area, and an early evening dinner of pheasant, trout, or buffalo steaks. As a result, the park is more than self-sufficient. In fiscal year 1995, Custer's revenues from user fees were ahead of expenses by $546,000.[3] The excess was used to modernize the park's waste treatment plant. That same year, nearby Wind Caves National Park lost $818,000 on its operation (U.S. Department of the Interior 1996).

Until very recently, enviro-capitalists found it difficult to compete with government's zero or below-market pricing of parks and recreation on federal lands. But that picture is changing because a growing number of people are dissatisfied with the crowds and deteriorating services. Increasingly, they are turning to opportunities on private lands where the crowds are smaller, and the quality of service is higher. While this speaks volumes for enviro-capitalists in the private sector, it illustrates a disturbing deficiency with federal lands. Making up one-third of the total land mass of the United States, these lands have tremendous potential for providing environmental amenities.

By following the lead of state land management and allowing federal land managers to collect realistic fees for amenity values and reinvest at least some of those fees in the resource, we can change the incentives faced by federal land managers. Toward that end, the 104th Congress took a first step. In 1996, legislation was passed with bipartisan support to allow some park managers on an experimental basis to raise entrance and user fees to more realistic levels. These parks will be able to keep 80 percent of the revenues they raise above the previous year and can use those revenues in the park where they are collected. This legislation puts parks on the way to stimulating entrepreneurship for the good of the parks and the treasury.

The Bad

In order for environmental entrepreneurs to act on their perceptions, they must be able to buy and sell rights to resources. Andrew Purkey of the Oregon Water Trust (chapter 5) would have little hope of saving salmon and steelhead habitat if he could not purchase or lease water rights. Piet Lamprecht would have little incentive to change his ranching operation in South Africa if he could not profit from turning the habitat over to wildlife (chapter 4). These enviro-capitalists gain from trade because there is something to buy (water rights for Purkey) or sell (hunting rights for Lamprecht). Unfortunately, government regulations can prevent buying and selling, especially when resources are publicly owned.

"Shocked and angered" was Alyson Heyrend's response to administrative law judge Ramon Child's ruling that the Nature Conservancy could not purchase and retire federal grazing permits. Heyrend works in the Great Basin Field Office of the conservancy, where in cooperation with the Rocky Mountain Elk Foundation, the conservancy put together a deal to buy the Cunningham Ranch in southeastern Utah. The groups paid $1.36 million for the 7,583-acre ranch, $180 per acre, a healthy sum for such arid land. But like all ranches in that area, the package includes grazing permits on 250,000 acres of adjacent public lands. The groups intended to continue paying the Bureau of Land Management (BLM) its annual grazing fee but not to continue grazing the land. However, Judge Child ruled that the BLM should cancel the unused grazing permits and sell them to other ranchers. He found conservancy's goals "laudable" but said that not using the permits subverts federal grazing policy.

Heyrend doesn't understand the decision. As she put it, "We have always worked within the system to achieve our goals. But now we're being told we have no role unless we graze cows." By working within the system, she means that the conservancy has been enviro-capitalist oriented, using willing buyer-willing seller transactions to obtain conservation easements or outright ownership of private property. Rather than simply calling for "no moo in '92" and "cattle free by '93," the Nature Conservancy has been willing to negotiate with ranchers to get cattle off public lands.

The ruling to disallow a halt to grazing stands in the way of enviro-capitalism. The conservancy also planned to purchase the S&H Ranch, one of the largest working cattle ranches in eastern Utah, again intending to retire the grazing permits. In this case they would have paid $2 million for 5,560 acres of private land and 164,000 acres of access to grazing on state and federal lands. The conservancy wanted to protect wildlife habitat in the rugged Book Cliffs, some 150 miles southeast of Salt Lake City. But the deal is off because the conservancy cannot retire the grazing permits. As Heyrend says, "If we cannot hold the grazing permits and the BLM gives them to someone else to run cattle, we could not then achieve our goal to manage the initiative for wildlife."

Similar results have occurred with state lands managed to generate revenues for public schools. Some environmental groups are willing to go head-to-head with ranchers when grazing leases are periodically renewed through auctions. For example, the Santa Fe-based Forest Guardians or the Idaho-based Idaho Watershed Project have outbid ranchers but still not gotten the leases. Forest Guardians was awarded a 2,000-acre lease on land that was too rocky for good grazing, but when it won the bid on "good" grazing land, it was denied the lease. John Horning, a spokesman for the group, said, "We just want to participate in the free market. We're not trying to use legal tools to shut people down. All we want is a level playing field."

When the Idaho group, "founded to identify and lease important watershed and riparian areas occurring on the school lands of the State of Idaho," bid $30 for grazing units in the Herd Creek Allotment, the local rancher, William Ingham, who had the permit, stated, "$30 is too much—we are not bidding." Ingham appealed the bid to the state land board, which by a 4–1 vote overturned the auction and awarded the lease to Ingham. The Idaho Watershed Project has had similar results on three other auctions. Because John Marvel, head of the project, has been so persistent, ranchers took their cause to the state legislature. In 1995, the legislature enacted the so-called "anti-Marvel bill" with the stated purpose of "encouraging a healthy Idaho livestock industry so as to generate related business and employment opportunities on a state and local level, thus supporting additional sales, income, and property taxes."[4] Later the same year, the state land board used the legislation's criteria to disqualify John Marvel and the Idaho Watershed Project as applicants for grazing leases.

When enviro-capitalists cannot engage in willing buyer-willing seller transactions, the potential for doing good is diminished. In the case of grazing permits, some environmental groups are willing to pay more than ranchers, indicating the potential for gains from trade. Clearly, in the Nature Conservancy case, ranchers gain or they would not sell, and the federal government continues to receive revenues equal to those from grazing. In the state cases, ranchers' grazing permits are less secure because they are shorter term and periodically put up for bid. If an environmental group wins the bid, the rancher loses the permit. Ranchers would like to eliminate the competition. But disallowing competing interests closes the market option to enviro-capitalists willing to put their money where their environmental amenities are. If they cannot work within the system as Alyson Heyrend said, their only option is to make the best of a bad situation and engage in acrimonious political battles.

The Ugly

"The heart of the last dusky seaside sparrow sits in a freezer in the genetics department of the University of Georgia," write Charles Mann and Mark Plummer (1992, 52). It died on 16 June 1987, twenty years after the U.S. Fish and Wildlife Service (FWS) placed it on the endangered species list. Its demise was to some a "signal failure of the Endangered Species Act" (Mann and Plummer 1992, 55). But actually it became extinct because the FWS, the agency charged with administering the Endangered Species Act, tried to save every listed species on a limited budget.

Ammodramus maritima nigrescens is one of nine subspecies of the sea-side sparrow species. This subspecies of bird had the smallest range of any North American bird. One population existed on a few thousand acres of marshland in Brevard County, Florida, and another was off-shore, on marshy Merritt Island.[5] Less than six inches in size, *A. m. nigrescens* nested only in treeless marsh grass areas.

When its habitat was reduced by draining marshes to increase pasture and the pesticides and water impoundments that were used to control mosquitos found their way into the food chain, the dusky sea-side sparrow population plummeted. By 1972 only two males could be found on Merritt Island, and a few hundred managed to survive on the mainland. Herbert Kale and Allan Cruickshank, two local ornithologists, concluded that the dusky was living on borrowed time unless some of the lands could be spared from conversion to pasture. They urged the FWS to buy out some of the ranchers, but their request left the agency with a dilemma, as described by Mann and Plummer:

> The agency now had to decide what it was going to do about the dusky. Was it going to lead the bird onto the ark, or strand it ashore? The choice was not easy. In 1969 Congress had appropriated $1.3 million for acquiring endangered species habitat. Several thousand acres of Florida swamp would cost more than a million dollars. Spending that money on *A. m. nigrescens* would mean not spending it on other equally desperate species. Should the Office of Endangered Species save the dusky and lose, say, the American alligator or the key deer? What Solomon could tell the agency which course to follow? (Mann and Plummer 1992, 55)

Ultimately, the FWS put most of its modest land acquisition budget into dusky habitat in Brevard County. In 1972, the agency purchased 2,000 acres of land for $787,000, and over the next four years, it purchased another 2,000 acres for $1 million.

What followed was a tragic comedy of errors. Despite its land purchases, the FWS failed to restore the area to habitat suitable for the dusky. In particular, it allowed further drainage of the land it purchased. Ranchers continued to burn areas, and a fire spread onto the FWS lands, burning three-quarters of the area and leaving little marsh grass for the dusky. By December 1975, only eleven males were left in the area. The agency bought another 1,500 acres but inexplicably again failed to prevent drainage on the lands.

By 1978, the government had spent $2.6 million for 6,200 acres to save the dusky seaside sparrow, but a FWS survey indicated that the remaining dusky population was on the brink of extinction. Only twenty-four males had survived, of which four remained on the burned-over area and twenty on the newly acquired land. None existed on Merritt Island.

In a desperate attempt to save a portion of the gene pool, Herbert Kale, the vice president for ornithology of the Florida Audubon Society, wanted to try captive breeding. Because no female sparrows had been known to exist after 1976, his approach called for breeding the remaining males with females from a closely related subspecies. Female hybrids could then be "back-crossed" to dusky males, producing birds that were three-quarters dusky. Continuing this process would mean the sixth generation would be 98.4 percent pure.

The FWS allowed Kale to capture the last five wild birds in 1979 and 1980. After successfully breeding a first generation of healthy, fertile hybrids, Kale contacted the service for permission to proceed with his breeding project. He fully expecting the service to give the go-ahead, but instead, he ran into a brick wall. "A new legal opinion said that the Endangered Species Act covered pure species only, and that federal money therefore could not be spent on hybrids. Despite an offer to fund the project privately, the service declared *A. m. nigrescens* off limits" (Mann and Plummer 1992, 58).

Several years elapsed without federal approval, but Kale remained dedicated to his task of saving the dusky. He arranged to work with curators at Walt Disney World's Discovery Island, with Disney picking up the tab. Finally, after two years of bureaucratic delays, another legal opinion allowed Kale to proceed. Unfortunately, nothing went right. Old age, incompatible pairings, failed nesting, and a series of accidents led to extinction of the sparrow.

Kale was bitter about the precious time that the project had lost due to bureaucratic bungling and lack of dedication. The service had paid lots of money for habitat that it had not managed properly. Unfortunately, even when somebody else was willing to pay, it had refused for several years to allow a last-ditch captive breeding effort. "The whole business was senseless and sad" (quoted in Mann and Plummer 1992, 59).

A stumbling block to environmental entrepreneurship is the failure of public institutions to rely more on the talents of enviro-capitalists than on bureaucracy. Such a position ignores the importance of entrepreneurship in generating new approaches to problems. Recall Rosalie Edge's success in ending a senseless slaughter of hawks at a time when there was a government bounty on their heads (chapter 3). Similarly,

E. A. McIlhenny of Tabasco pepper sauce fame used his own money and land to help save the snowy egret (chapter 3). Unfortunately, the Fish and Wildlife Service hampered the innovative effort of Herbert Kale to save the dusky seaside sparrow.

Given the fiscal constraints on federal agencies, some environmental entrepreneurship is certainly called for. A 1990 report from the Office of the Inspector General estimated the recovery costs over a ten-year period at $4.6 billion for all endangered species in the United States currently listed or expected to be listed. That same year, the FWS budget for endangered species research, recovery planning, and land acquisition was $10.6 million. Other agencies provide support, but even so, the total budget for species recovery in 1990 was $102 million, less than one-fourth of the annual amount estimated by the inspector general.

To make matters worse, government subsidies provide another source of perverse incentives. Subsidized water projects provide a quintessential example (see Anderson and Snyder 1997). Dams on every major river system in the West, except the Yellowstone River, home of the paddlefish discussed in chapter 1, have benefited irrigation interests while the costs have fallen on taxpayers and the environment. Moreover, most projects fail to pass benefit-cost analysis tests of economic feasibility. Most recently, funds were appropriated for the Central Utah Project although it would cost $400 per acre-foot to deliver water to farms where it would be worth $30 per acre-foot and where farmers would pay $8 per acre-foot (Anderson and Snyder 1997).

These subsidized water projects have exacted a heavy toll on fish and wildlife. Dams built along the Columbia River and its tributaries, for example, have effectively blocked fish migrations and inundated spawning areas. As a result, anadromous fisheries in the Pacific Northwest are declining and, in some cases, are on the verge of extinction. The plight of Pacific Northwest salmon and steelhead is a tragic by-product of the federal government's effort to make the "desert bloom like a rose" (Reisner 1986). In 1991, the American Fisheries Society's endangered species committee identified 214 native naturally spawning Pacific salmon and steelhead populations that were in trouble, and of these, 101 were at risk of extinction (Nehlson, Williams, and Lichatowich 1991).

As a result of federal water projects, wild salmon runs in Washington, Oregon, Idaho, and northern California now number in the thousands and hundreds, where once they were in the millions. Idaho's

Snake River wild sockeye salmon run is on the brink of extinction. The first population to be officially protected as a threatened species under the Endangered Species Act was the Sacramento River chinook. Between 1967 and 1969, the winter chinook run averaged 86,509 adults in the upper reach of the Sacramento River, but it plummeted to a historical low of 550 adults in 1989 (Nehlson, Williams, and Lichatowich 1991).

The estimated taxpayer cost of Pacific salmon recovery is billions of dollars (Herr 1994). After fish ladders were built to allow salmon and steelhead to negotiate dams, fish biologists discovered that young fish had trouble finding their way through the reservoirs behind the dams without the current to guide them. Hence, reservoir levels are being drawn down to provide more current, but this reduces water availability for agriculture and recreation. Alternatively, fish are trucked around or barged through reservoirs at enormous cost. In the end, these measures may cost more than $900 per salmon saved. At the same time, enviro-capitalists at the Oregon Water Trust and the Environmental Defense Fund are taking incremental steps toward salmon recovery with water markets (chapter 5). They could do much more if both federal and state governments removed bureaucratic and legal roadblocks to their entrepreneurial efforts (Leal 1994). These examples are ugly because they represent a senseless destruction of natural amenities fostered by our political institutions.

Going for the Good

In the 1930s, Aldo Leopold became the American conservation movement's "voice in the wilderness" because he was one of the few who understood the importance of environmental entrepreneurship. Unlike so many in the movement who were putting all their eggs in the public stewardship basket, Leopold began espousing the need to balance wildlife policy by enlisting the services of the private landowner. He predicted that "conservation will ultimately boil down to rewarding the private landowner who conserves the public interest" (Leopold 1991, 202). He recognized that the private landowner was critical to the recovery of wildlife populations and that in conservation as in business, incentives really do matter. He knew that farmers and ranchers had to survive financially and urged that we create an institutional environment favorable to private stewardship. Unfortunately, contemporary government policies continue to tilt the playing field away from private amenity production and decidedly toward public provision, where entrepreneurship is currently lacking.[6]

Regardless of the resource in question, the key to entrepreneurship is secure private property rights coupled with the freedom to contract. Tom Bourland could change timber management for a major timber corporation because the company owned its land and could contract with hunters, fishermen, and recreational users who were willing to pay International Paper for access to the amenities (chapter 1). Zach Willey can enhance stream flows as long as he can contract with holders of water rights to reduce their diversions (chapter 5). The White Mountain Apache can manage their elk herd for quality hunting because, for all intents and purposes, they own the animals within the reservation (chapter 8).

Even where property rights are clearly defined and enforced, however, enviro-capitalists must specify contractual terms and then monitor the contract. Bourland had to specify what International Paper was supplying to hunters and recreational users and what was expected from them in return. He had to discover the price people were willing to pay and work with timber managers to supply the environmental amenities. Willey had to specify what he wanted from water users and what he was willing to supply in return. Because he was not marketing the water directly to those who demand salmon and steelhead habitat, he had to discover a secondary market in electric power production that allowed him to muster the financial resources to compensate farmers for forgone water use. In both Bourland's and Willey's cases, the contract had to be monitored to ensure that the goods were delivered.

Especially on the entrepreneurial frontier, specifying and monitoring the contract is costly because the inputs and outputs are nontraditional; that is, land and water owners are not accustomed to marketing their resources for new environmental uses. It is one thing to lease land for commodity production, such as timber harvesting, where the output and its value are well known, but it is quite another to do so for wildlife habitat, where the requirements for producing wildlife habitat are not well known and people are not accustomed to purchasing this good through the market.

These costs of specifying and monitoring contracts—transaction costs, as economists call them—increase with the number of parties to the contract and can be sufficiently high to prevent private solutions. For example, consider the difficulty of providing habitat for a species such as elk, caribou, or waterfowl, which requires a large territory to roam freely (see Lueck 1995). On the Fort Apache Reservation or on

Ted Turner's huge ranch, it is easier to coordinate the provision of habitat because the managers do not have to contract with other landowners. In both cases, the land areas are large enough to accommodate the requirements of the wildlife.

But the contractual problems are greater if providing the habitat necessitates contracting with tens if not hundreds of landowners, each with a small share of the land required. With transaction costs much higher, the feasibility of privately providing wildlife habitat declines. The entrepreneur will only be able to cover the higher contracting costs of amassing land for wildlife habitat if the value of the wildlife is extremely high.[7]

Transaction costs also may make it difficult to get people to pay for environmental goods. For example, if people enjoy viewing wildlife and can do so from a public road, a private provider would have to erect a high fence to exclude nonpayers. This is what zoos do, but the cost of exclusion is not trivial, and the nature of the good almost certainly changes because seeing an animal in a zoo is not the same as seeing it in the wild. To the extent that the cost of excluding nonpaying customers is high, people can ride free on the efforts of the entrepreneur to provide wildlife habitat. The result is that providers of environmental goods will be undercompensated relative to what people are willing to pay, thus making it more difficult to generate private entrepreneurship.

High contracting costs and the free-rider problem are classic reasons for governmental provision of environmental amenities. Governmental agencies may control land areas large enough to accommodate migrating species, and where they do not, the agencies can use the powers of government to regulate private landowners to provide wildlife habitat. The government's power to tax provides a way of overcoming the free-rider problem.

But it will not do to assert that the government's *potential* for overcoming the contracting cost problems faced by enviro-capitalists is sufficient to guarantee that it will do a better job of providing amenities. For just as there are costs of specifying and monitoring private contracts, there are costs of specifying and monitoring what governmental agencies do (Anderson and Leal 1991, 19–20). How do agencies know what amenities the public wants, and how does the public know whether the agency is providing them? What are the incentives faced by bureaucrats? Will their entrepreneurship be switched on to produce what the constituents want or will it be channeled to maximizing bureaucratic budgets? These are questions that all too often are not asked.

Even if government can lower certain transaction costs through political land ownership, taxation, and regulation, it can raise other transaction costs. For example, legal constraints on the ability of irrigators to sell or lease their water rights to enviro-capitalists raise transaction costs and reduce the potential for private entrepreneurial solutions. Restrictions on hunting markets make it more difficult for landowners to profit from providing wildlife habitat. Governmental regulation can undermine the security of property rights and thwart entrepreneurship. The quintessential example is the Endangered Species Act, which actually penalizes landowners whose lands harbor wildlife by restricting the activities from which owners can profit.

Without private property rights and contracting, enviro-capitalists are forced to seek political methods to achieve their ends. If water cannot be sold or leased by irrigators to environmental groups interested in maintaining or increasing stream flows, those groups will have little alternative but to seek regulations that guarantee minimum flows. If ivory cannot be marketed through legitimate channels, poaching will be the only way that people can turn elephants from a liability into an asset.

As environmental amenities become more valuable, it will be difficult to stifle enviro-capitalists who see opportunities for new and better ways to achieve environmental ends while making a profit. Indeed, over the past few years, especially as federal budgets have tightened and environmental regulations have been limited by "takings" proceedings, environmentalists have risen to the challenge with new market solutions—hence the cases in this book.

Whether the ground broken by the enviro-capitalists featured here will prove fertile for the next generation of environmental entrepreneurs depends on the institutional environment that generation inherits. As the lowering of the Iron Curtain showed, pure socialism provides ugly results. Mixed management of resources, such as federal land management, national parks, and federal water projects, is somewhat better, but the results are still bad. To harness the forces of enviro-capitalism, we must use market incentives and allow enviro-capitalists to do good for the environment.

Notes

1. These comments were made by Barbee during a question-and-answer period following a speech he gave on Yellowstone Park at Montana State University, Bozeman, Montana, 28 October 1987.

2. By law, national forests are managed to achieve the "combination [of land uses] that will best meet the needs of the American people . . . and not necessarily the combination of uses that will give the greatest dollar return or the greatest unit output (Multiple-Use Sustained-Yield Act, 16 U.S.C. § 531 (a) [1988]).

3. Fax from Roger Bamsey, Custer State Park employee, on budget and expenditures for the fiscal year, 2 April 1996.

4. Senate Bill 1194, sec. 58-310.

5. In the 1950s, NASA acquired Merritt Island, but the northern part of the island was turned into Merritt Island National Wildlife Refuge.

6. An exception in recent years has been the conservation reserve program. Over 36 million acres of highly erodible land has been taken out of production. The program is a very expensive "Band-Aid" to past farm policies that encouraged farmers to plant on marginal land. See Leal (1990).

7. Even in this case, private action is not out of the question as evidenced by the nonprofit Rocky Mountain Elk Foundation's efforts to raise private funds to lease or purchase habitat in more densely populated areas.

References

Anderson, Terry L., and Donald R. Leal. 1991. *Free Market Environmentalism*. San Francisco: Pacific Research Institute for Public Policy.

Anderson, Terry L., and Pamela Snyder. 1997. *In Search of Water Markets: Priming the Invisible Pump*. Washington, DC: Cato Institute.

Herr, Andrew. 1994. Saving the Snake River Salmon: Are We Solving the Right Problem? Working paper 94-15. Bozeman, MT: Political Economy Research Center.

Leal, Donald R. 1990. A Bird's-eye View of Destructive Farm Policy. *Wall Street Journal*, March 1.

———. 1994. Let Rights to Water Be Traded. *Idaho Statesman*, June 5.

———. 1995. Turning a profit on public forests. *PERC Policy Series*, PS-4. Bozeman, MT: Political Economy Research Center.

Leopold, Aldo. 1991. Conservation economics [1934]. In *The River of the Mother of God and Other Essays by Aldo Leopold*, ed. Susan L. Flader and J. Baird Callicott. Madison: University of Wisconsin Press, 193–202.

Leuck, Dean. 1995. The Economic Organization of Wildlife Institutions. In *Wildlife in the Marketplace*, ed. Terry L. Anderson and Peter J. Hill. Lanham, MD: Rowman and Littlefield Publishers, 1–24.

Mann, Charles C., and Mark L. Plummer. 1992. The Butterfly Problem. *Atlantic Monthly*, January, 47–70.

McMillion, Scott. 1992. The (Nearly) Invisible Timber Sale. *Bozeman Daily Chronicle*, March 20.

Milstein, Michael. 1996. Park Will Close Campground and Two Museums. *Billings Gazette*, April 16.

Nehlson, Willa, Jack E. Williams, and James A. Lichatowich. 1991. Pacific Salmon at the Crossroads: Stocks at Risk from California, Oregon, Idaho, and Washington. *Fisheries* 16(2): 6–7.

Reisner, Mark. 1986. *Cadillac Desert: The American West and Its Disappearing Water*. New York: Viking Penguin.

U.S. Department of Interior. National Park Service, Budget Division. 1996. *United States Department of the Interior Budget Justifications, FY 1997*. Washington, DC: U.S. Department of the Interior.

Index

About the Authors

Terry L. Anderson is professor of economics at Montana State University and executive director of PERC (the Political Economy Research Center) in Bozeman, Montana. Anderson is the series editor of PERC's Political Economy Forum Series published by Rowman & Littlefield. He is coauthor with Donald Leal of *Free Market Environmentalism* and author or editor of seventeen other books. His most recent books include *Sovereign Nations or Reservations? An Economic History of American Indians* and *Water Marketing: The Next Generation*, which he coedited with Peter J. Hill. He has published numerous articles in professional journals and popular publications as diverse as the *Wall Street Journal* and *Fly Fisherman*. Anderson has been a visiting scholar at Oxford University, the University of Basel (Switzerland), Canterbury University (New Zealand), Stanford University, and Cornell University Law School. He holds a B.S. in business administration from the University of Montana and an M.S. and Ph.D. in economics from the University of Washington.

Donald R. Leal is a senior associate of PERC, in Bozeman, Montana. He is coauthor with Anderson of *Free Market Environmentalism*, which received the 1992 Choice Outstanding Academic Book Award. He is a contributing author in *Multiple Conflicts Over Multiple Uses*, *Taking the Environment Seriously*, and *Taking Ownership: Property Rights in Fisheries*. Over the last eleven years, Leal has published numerous articles on fisheries, water, recreation, oil and gas, timber, and federal land use policy. His articles appear in newspapers such as the *Wall Street Journal*, *New York Times*, and *Chicago Tribune*, as well as specialized journals. Leal's recent studies comparing federal and state management of public forests have fostered a new perspective on public land management. Leal has a B.S. in mathematics and an M.S. in statistics from California State University at Hayward.